ADVANCE PRAISE FOR
GLOWING BUNNIES!?

" This important easy-to-read book vividly demonstrates why animal welfare must guide genetic engineering, whether for science, medicine, agriculture, or conservation. There are many important ethical questions that require us to dig deeply into why we are engaging in these experiments and who really benefits. Such as, Are we making animal lives better or only our own lives? Are we acting with care, respect, and compassion? Entertaining, thoughtful, and packed with information, these stories should be required reading because genetic engineering is rapidly becoming business as usual."

— DR. MARC BEKOFF, PROFESSOR EMERITUS OF ECOLOGY AND EVOLUTIONARY BIOLOGY, UNIVERSITY OF COLORADO, BOULDER, COAUTHOR OF *THE ANIMALS' AGENDA* AND *A DOG'S WORLD: IMAGINING THE LIVES OF DOGS IN A WORLD WITHOUT HUMANS*

GLOWING BUNNIES!?

WHY WE'RE MAKING HYBRIDS, CHIMERAS, AND CLONES

JEFF CAMPBELL

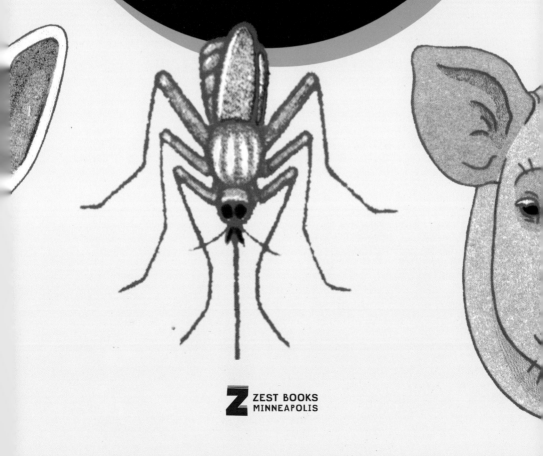

Z ZEST BOOKS
MINNEAPOLIS

TO ALL CREATURES GREAT AND SMALL, PAST, PRESENT, AND FUTURE . . .

Zest Books™
An imprint of Lerner Publishing Group, Inc.
241 First Avenue North
Minneapolis, MN 55401 USA

For reading levels and more information, look up this title at www.lernerbooks.com.
Visit us at zestbooks.net.

Cover and chapter opener illustrations by Greer Stothers.
Diagram on p. 70 by Laura K. Westlund.

Designed by Lindsey Owens.
Main body text set in Adobe Garamond Pro Regular.
Typeface provided by Adobe Systems.

Library of Congress Cataloging-in-Publication Data

Names: Campbell, Jeff (Jeff Logan), author.
Title: Glowing bunnies!? : why we're making hybrids, chimeras, and clones / by Jeff Campbell.
Description: Minneapolis : Zest Books, [2021] | Includes bibliographical references and index. | Audience: Ages 11–18 | Audience: Grades 7–9 | Summary: "Bioengineering has the potential to solve a range of urgent, global problems. Glowing Bunnies!? introduces teen readers to the possibilities, dangers, and ethical issues involved in bioengineering"— Provided by publisher.
Identifiers: LCCN 2020018694 (print) | LCCN 2020018695 (ebook) | ISBN 9781541599291 (library binding) | ISBN 9781541599307 (paperback) | ISBN 9781728419152 (ebook)
Subjects: LCSH: Bioengineering—Moral and ethical aspects—Juvenile literature. | Genetic engineering—Moral and ethical aspects—Juvenile literature. | Bioethics—Juvenile literature.
Classification: LCC TA164 .C35 2021 (print) | LCC TA164 (ebook) | DDC 179/.3—dc23

LC record available at https://lccn.loc.gov/2020018694
LC ebook record available at https://lccn.loc.gov/2020018695

Manufactured in the United States of America
1-48203-48775-11/10/2021

CONTENTS

THE POSSIBILITIES ARE ENDLESS

Welcome to our brave new world.

With genetic engineering, our science-fiction future has arrived. Every time people have imagined some impossible creation—a Frankenstein's monster or clone army, reborn dinosaurs or bioengineered sharks, mutant insects, supersmart chimpanzees, or even the ancient mythic Chimera, that part-lion, part-goat, part-serpent, fire-breathing beast—we've wondered, *What if it really existed?*

In one way or another, if not today, then tomorrow, we may get to find out. These flights of fancy could come to life—and all thanks to our new genetic tools, which allow us to modify and change animals in almost any way we want.

This illustration depicts a bronze sculpture of a chimera built in 400 B.C.E. In Greek mythology, the Chimera terrorized the countryside of Lycia in Anatolia or Asia Minor until it was defeated by the hero Bellerophon and his winged steed Pegasus.

Spider goats and glowing bunnies? Yep, they exist, and you'll meet them in these pages.

Mind-controlled rats, double-muscled dogs, de-extinced aurochs, ligers, pizzlies, cloned cattle, super pigs? Come say hello.

Woolly mammoths and dinosaurs? Self-destructing mosquitoes? Human-animal chimeras? Monkeys with humanized brains? Brand-new organisms made from scratch?

All in the works.

Of course, this newfound ability freaks many people out. Wouldn't it be better if certain fictional creatures stayed fictional?

As a society, that's what we need to talk about. Genetic engineering is quickly becoming routine, an everyday fact of life. Scientists have learned not only how to read the genetic book of life but how to write and speak its language. If we use this power wisely—this incredible ability to reshape animals, plants, and ourselves, remixing anything with DNA—we might solve some of the biggest problems facing us, other species, and the environment. Indeed, this powerful technology is poised to transform our world . . .

In movies, when someone talks like this—*we have the power to transform the world!*—you know some tagalong character, the film's plucky comic relief, is going to raise a trembling hand and ask, *So, um, is this really a good idea?*

Does anyone ever listen?

This book is that character. This book raises a hand to ask, Given what we *can* do, what *should* we do? This book presents some of the genetically engineered animals scientists are making and asks you to consider which of these projects seem like wise, practical, and safe ways to use this technology to improve our world, and which might be, you know, not so smart after all.

Each of us, individually and collectively, needs to raise a hand and ask these questions because how we answer them will determine our future.

Good science fiction always tells a cautionary tale. It asks "what if?" and then speculates about what could happen—usually by imagining all the ways things could go wrong. With genetic engineering, scientists don't need to ask "what if?" anymore. Almost anything is becoming possible.

The only question left is, Why not?

THE ANTHROPOCENE: A WORLD SHAPED BY US

The first reason scientists and researchers typically give for using genetic engineering is curiosity. Because we can. That's how it's always been. If humans *can* do something, we try it out. The curiosity to discover how life works is what drives all science, and many bioengineering projects start with the itch to answer the question, What would happen if we altered life *this way?*

As you'll see, these experiments have revealed a great deal about the way life, and genetics, work. Of course, sometimes scientists pursue genetic engineering with a specific goal in mind, but either way, the questions that motivate researchers tend to be similar: Could this new creation or being serve a useful purpose? How might we use our new tools and knowledge to help solve problems, repair damage, and improve our existence?

This is where things get complicated, and no single book could cover all the possibilities. *Glowing Bunnies!?* focuses primarily on animals (not plants, microorganisms, or humans). It describes how and why people are modifying animals and explores some of the issues this raises. Here is what you will find in this book:

Part 1 focuses on animal conservation and the extinction crisis. Because of human impacts, habitat destruction, and climate change, more and more wild species are becoming endangered and going extinct, but by using genetic engineering, we might help wild species survive.

Part 2 considers how we might help restore damaged ecosystems and environments and even combat climate change by "de-extincting" lost species or creating new animals to release into the wild.

Part 3 looks at the challenges facing agriculture and how to feed ourselves without further harming the planet. Genetic engineering could make agriculture more efficient and less polluting while also improving the health and welfare of livestock.

Of course, we use animals in countless ways: to do jobs, make products, and share our lives as animal companions. Part 4 considers all of this but especially pets.

Finally, part 5 focuses on human health and medicine, or using genetically engineered animals to help fight or eliminate disease, heal people, and directly save lives.

If there's any problem anywhere involving living things, you can bet that someone somewhere is working furiously to solve it using genetic engineering. Whether these efforts will succeed the way people intend remains to be seen, but in ways large and small, people are urgently trying to use genetic engineering to reshape our world—and not just for our benefit but for the benefit of the entire planet.

—Hand waving in the air.—

That sounds great except for this: many people would say that human impacts and tinkering with nature are what have caused most of these problems—or at least made them worse. And given all the messes humans have made over the years, it's easy to conclude that we aren't very good at tinkering. What makes scientists, researchers, or anyone think new tools will help us do any better? Shouldn't we learn our lesson and stop?

As it is, human impacts on Earth have become so extreme, all-encompassing, and enduring that people struggle to properly characterize them. Some geologists even suggest we rename the current geological epoch after ourselves. Epoch names reflect the defining force shaping the world, and over the last few centuries, as one essay notes,

"[Humans] are like an asteroid strike. We have the impact of an ice age." Or perhaps a Thanos finger snap. In a geological instant, humans are causing waves of extinctions, changes to species, and upheaval in nature. *Anthropo* is Greek for "human," so some scientists suggest we call our time the Anthropocene.

As evolutionary biologist Chris Thomas writes, "We are living on a fundamentally human-altered planet, and there is no longer any such thing as human-free nature."

In other words, we have *already* transformed our world so radically and extensively that not doing anything isn't really an option anymore. If we want to solve a particular problem or heal the damage we've caused, often our only choice is to *keep* transforming the world using every tool we have. While genetic engineering isn't always the best or only option, we can't avoid making decisions. Even choosing not to act has consequences.

Science journalist M. R. O'Connor writes, "Humans are in the midst of an unplanned experiment of influencing the evolution of the planet's biodiversity. . . . And which animals we prioritize, and how we choose to save them, tinkers with the biosphere as a whole."

Stewart Brand—the cofounder of Revive & Restore, which is helping de-extinct the passenger pigeon—captures this dilemma even more dramatically: "We are as gods and *have* to get good at it."

Sure, Brand sounds like a Hollywood-ready mad scientist. But he describes the situation well. Genetic engineering has given us the power to alter life as we see fit, and if we decide to use it, we must get good at it.

GENETIC ENGINEERING: NEW TOOLS FOR AN OLD GAME

What exactly *is* genetic engineering? It often sounds like magic: a scientist tinkers with the unseen, swirls a beaker, and—*poof!*—a new creature is born.

In fact, tinkering with genes is how evolution works. Organisms are built to change as a way to survive, and through genetic change, species evolve into new forms. In essence, as the world changes—as, say, climates shift or as new diseases, threats, or opportunities arise— animals adjust by moving, mating, or behaving differently, and their genes respond to transform their bodies.

As a rule, these changes are usually small and happen very slowly. Yet eventually, this is how one species can diverge into many species— with, say, some animals becoming bears and others skunks, wolves, and walruses. Sometimes, only a little genetic change can lead to radical physical differences. Humans and mice diverged a long time ago and appear unalike, but their *genomes*—their genetic blueprints—are about 90 percent the same.

That's a pretty good magic trick. And nature tinkers with every animal that's born. Each individual (except a clone, more on that later) is a unique mix of two genomes: their parents'. Every human child is also born with about a hundred genetic mutations that don't exist in either parent.

These mutations rarely do anything, but they show that nothing is actually magical about genetic change. Just the opposite: by tweaking virtually the same material, life has conjured people, mice, and elephants, dinosaurs and birds, and this process continues. All species are constantly changing, even if it happens too gradually for us to notice.

Then we did notice it.

This remarkable, even unsettling fact of life became obvious when certain wolves that had chosen to live with humans were clearly not wolves anymore. These wolves looked and behaved differently, and so we gave them a new name—dogs. Dogs were the world's first domestic species.

This happened at least fourteen thousand years ago, and after that, we started selectively breeding animals (and plants) on purpose, creating more domestic species. Crossbreeding and selective breeding, or deliberately mating certain animals so they produce offspring with the traits we prefer, are forms of genetic engineering. In the broadest sense, *genetic engineering* is any deliberate manipulation of nature that leads to genetic change—and we've been doing it for millennia.

However, selective breeding is slow, inefficient, and even chaotic. Complete genomes mix in unpredictable ways. Using selective breeding to deliberately shape an animal to consistently possess the traits we want takes many, many generations. It's like shaking a house to rearrange the living room furniture. Occasionally, the couch will end up where we want, but not every time, and other things shift too.

Gene-editing technology, in contrast, is direct, fast, and extremely precise. We can identify and change the exact genes that affect the specific traits we want, without touching or "moving" anything else. If we want to adjust only the couch—or modify a single trait—we can. *Presto!*

To be more precise: what makes gene-editing technology different—different from evolution and different from selective breeding—is that our new tools can alter the DNA in a cell directly, and they can alter DNA in ways that nature can't.

This difference is revolutionary. And even though these tools are almost brand-new and we are still learning how genes work, scientists are already using biotechnology to revolutionize life. Here is a quick list of some of the amazing things we can do: We can sequence a being's entire genome, writing out its DNA like a book of genetic instructions. Within that book, we can locate specific genes (sequences of DNA, akin to how a word is made of letters) and identify what physical, inherited traits they produce or influence. We can alter, remove, or add individual genes or portions of genes. We can cut-and-paste genes (or portions of genes) between one plant or animal and any other

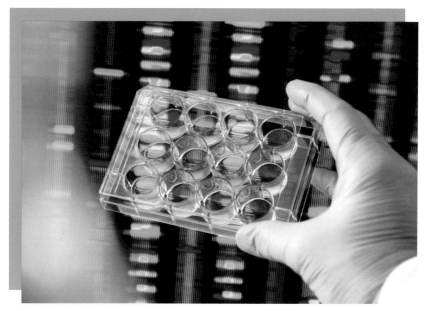

Over the last fifty years, bioengineering technology has become so exact, particularly the gene-editing tool CRISPR-Cas9, that scientists can modify any DNA and even write new strands from scratch.

plant or animal (like moving words between books). With cloning, we can replicate an entire genome exactly. We can use recovered, reconstructed, or frozen DNA to clone or re-create extinct species. We can write new, synthetic DNA sequences letter by letter (like inventing new words). And we can write entire *new books*, mixing and rearranging any DNA—both existing and synthetic—to create never-before-seen organisms that nature could never produce.

Yet this book isn't really about technology, not in itself. The goal isn't to teach you how to use these tools or how to become a bioengineer. This book explores the ways we are genetically altering animals and asks you to consider whether these projects seem like good ideas. Thankfully, we don't need a bioengineering degree to understand what bioengineering does, and we don't need to invent a gene-editing tool to make smart decisions about how to use it.

THE TINKERER'S DILEMMA: DECIDING WHAT TO DO

In 2020 the Nobel Prize in Chemistry was awarded to Jennifer Doudna and Emmanuelle Charpentier for their coinvention in 2012 of the gene-editing tool CRISPR-Cas9 (clustered regularly interspaced short palindromic repeats). For a brief description of how this tool works, see pages 69–70. Göran Hansson, the secretary-general of the Royal Swedish Academy of Sciences, who announced the award, put it succinctly: "This year's prize is about rewriting the code of life."

CRISPR is so precise and easy to use, and its potential is so limitless, that it has been almost instantly adopted by nearly every genetics lab around the world. Doudna says, "It was really a curiosity-driven project from the beginning." Doudna and Charpentier simply wanted to see if they could harness and program one of the body's own mechanisms for making genetic edits, and their curiosity is currently transforming science and our collective future.

"It's kind of an awesome thing to think about, the power to control the evolution of our species. It's something that in the not-too-distant past would have been unimaginable," says Doudna. "I'm deeply committed to democratizing technology . . . so that it's available and accessible to people that need it." However, "it's critical to ensure that the technology is used safely and effectively."

Just the phrase "control evolution" conjures visions of *Jurassic Park*: mixing genes and unleashing catastrophe. But while science fiction loves stories of mad scientists "playing god" in secret labs, scientists in real life want people to understand their work and public consensus about what to do.

They are also cautious, since they know as well as anyone how powerful their tools are. This is why most scientists say we should abide by the precautionary principle: if we don't know what the impacts of gene editing or a modified animal will be, we should not use, eat, or release that creature. We must first study and test genetic modifications to ensure they are safe for ourselves and for animals. As in medicine, the first rule is do no harm.

Caution helps minimize risk, but it never eliminates risk entirely. We still need to ask nitty-gritty questions to decide what to do in any situation. As the old saying goes, the devil is in the details. When it comes to gene editing, one of the first things to evaluate is who benefits: people, animals, or both? Do we hope to save species from extinction, improve animal health, or improve an entire ecosystem that will affect many species? Or is bioengineering animals meant mainly to benefit us, such as to improve human life or health?

Changing animals for our own benefit isn't necessarily wrong, nor is engineering nature—we've always done both. Altered animals can be used in multiple ways and have multiple impacts, good and bad. Sometimes, genetic engineering might be justified for some reasons or in some situations but not for others. Or genetic engineering alone might fail to solve a problem if we don't also adjust human behavior, attitudes, regulations, or laws.

As you read this book, consider these three types of concerns:

1. Is it practical? Is it an effective solution for the problem? What is the cost—in time, money, effort, and animal welfare—and are the benefits worth it? Is the promised good greater than any potential harm or danger? Are there other, perhaps less risky ways to achieve the same thing?

2. Will people and society accept it? Does society agree on the problem *and* the solution? Could public rejection cause failure? To succeed, do we need to revise our laws or regulations? Will it be difficult for us to live or coexist with a new animal?

3. Is the altered animal healthy? Will genetic changes cause the animal pain or suffering? Could other species be negatively affected? To the best of our ability, are we caring for the animals we're making?

These might sound like simple, yes-or-no questions, but they aren't. They are very complex, and even if this book tried, it couldn't answer them all. This book can't even pose all the questions that each situation raises. Instead, this book's goal is to start discussions. Hopefully, these stories will help you understand what scientists and researchers are doing and what they hope to achieve. Then you can begin to evaluate these efforts for yourself. Genetic engineering is full of promise, hope, and incredible opportunity, but it's forcing us to consider issues we've never faced before.

FRANKENSTEIN'S LESSON: CARING FOR OUR CREATIONS

In Mary Shelley's novel *Frankenstein*, the naive scientist Victor Frankenstein stitches a new human out of spare parts. He believes his creation will be beautiful and loved, but the creature turns out hideous, and Victor rejects him as a "monster." People react with disgust and fear and drive the creature away. So the creature—unaccepted, alone, aware of what he is, and filled with suffering—takes revenge by (*spoiler alert!*) killing the people Frankenstein loves.

This is a common theme in science fiction. Many stories about bioengineering are allegorical warnings: They dramatize fears that genetic engineering is inherently wrong, that it creates monsters who will hurt us. Sometimes, stories embody a belief that tinkering with genes is literally "playing god," and so God will punish us through our "unnatural" creations.

In a way, this book is a collection of Frankenstein stories. These new animals—which wouldn't exist without our tinkering—blur lines in ways that can make us uncomfortable. They defy our categories and definitions between what is natural and unnatural, what is one species or another, what is human and not human, what is right and wrong.

For example, we domesticated cattle from wild aurochs, and we accept this type of genetic engineering. Cattle seem natural. We don't

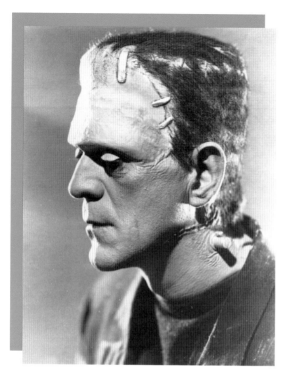

The 1931 movie adaptation of Shelley's novel depicts Dr. Frankenstein's creature with a flat head, scalp staples, and bolts fastened to the neck. These attributes aren't in the book, but they evoke the horror we are meant to feel toward a reanimated person.

fear or reject them. So if we use gene editing to alter cows so they don't grow horns, is that "unnatural"? Does directly altering their genetics turn their milk and meat into Frankenfood—something we should fear, something that might hurt us?

Is a glowing bunny a "monster" or just a new kind of rabbit, one we'd happily keep as a pet?

Individually and collectively, we need to ask these difficult, even uncomfortable questions and figure out where to draw the line.

But there is another way to interpret the Frankenstein story, one that provides a useful ethical guide whenever we tinker with animals. When Frankenstein creates a new person—whether that is right or wrong—his real mistake is to reject and abandon that being. Eventually, the creature confronts Frankenstein, and he asks the scientist to make another being like himself, a female companion to be his wife. Frankenstein is horrified and refuses, and this is what drives his creation to revenge. Without Frankenstein's cruelty and rejection, maybe *Frankenstein* would have had a happy ending.

For genetic engineering, this means, whatever we make and for whatever reason, we should always care for our creations. Then we might avoid causing new or even worse problems than the ones we were originally trying to solve. Frankenstein's "monster" only wants what all beings want: the ability to be happy on their own terms, avoid pain, be healthy, have companionship, and reproduce. Ideally, bioengineered animals should be no worse off and, hopefully, better than they were before.

Animals also have minds. They can make choices and will try to satisfy their needs. We may struggle to understand the inner lives of animals, but we know this much. And we know that certain species—particularly great apes, elephants, dolphins, dogs, and others—are highly intelligent, emotional, social, conscious, and even self-aware beings.

They are not the same as us, of course, but they don't need to be for us to treat them with compassion.

So . . . let's meet the new animals of the future—the altered ones who might help us save our world.

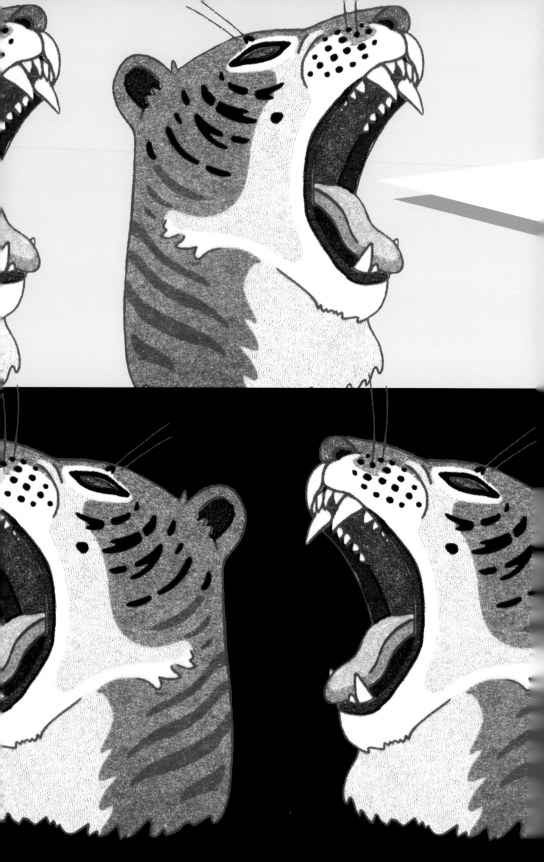

PART 1
WILD NATURE 2.0

Lions and rhinos lord the grassland. Wolves and tigers rule the forest. These awe-inspiring creatures epitomize wilderness, and through conservation, we seek to preserve them and nature just as they are.

What if we can't?

What if we shouldn't?

What if the only way to conserve wild species and natural habitats is to change them?

That's our dilemma. No place on Earth, no species, remains untouched by human impacts and climate change, which are causing a crisis. But the more we tinker with nature, the more it raises fundamental questions: What is wild? What is natural? What is a species?

This is the focus of part 1: how we are altering animals to save species. We can't save every species, and some are evolving before our eyes, whether we like it or not. In a way, conservation asks, Which species should we fight for, and how?

In the end, the decisions we make will be our collective answer to the biggest question of all: What kind of world do we want to live in?

21

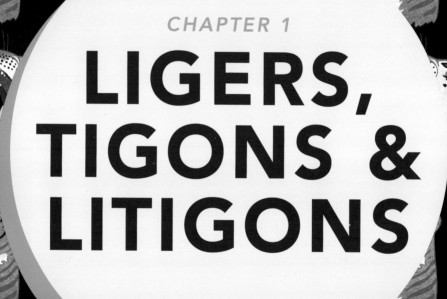

CHAPTER 1

LIGERS, TIGONS & LITIGONS

Among wild species, lions are the only social cats. They hunt by day in female-led packs in wide-open savannas, their tawny fur blending seamlessly into tall, dry grasses.

Tigers are solitary. They live alone and hunt in forests at night, and their black-and-orange stripes are perfect camouflage in the dappled jungle.

These species used to share habitat across the Middle East, but today the only place where they might meet is a tiny patch of forest in India.

No one ever sees them together. As different species, they live entirely separate lives. Their common ancestor lived about 4.6 million years ago, and until about 200 years ago, people believed that a lion-tiger hybrid was impossible.

BIRTH OF THE FRANKENCATS

Perhaps it was an accident. A careless keeper left a male lion and a tigress together in the same cage, and instead of attacking each other, they mated, conceived a child, and voilà! A liger was born.

Ligers are giant hybrids who seamlessly blend the features of both lions and tigers. This has long made them popular attractions for zoos and wildlife parks.

23

Historians don't know when exactly this happened, but the first art depicting ligers appeared in the 1820s. In the 1830s, two miraculous liger cubs were presented to England's royal family. By then, savvy zookeepers were deliberately crossbreeding lions and tigers to make more.

Naturalists and the public were fascinated. Ligers shouldn't exist, yet they did and still do. They are a magical blend of both parents—with faint striping and modest manes, a lionlike tail and a tiger's love of water. They are also gigantic, bigger than either parent. Adults can be more than 10 feet (3 m) long and weigh over 800 pounds (363 kg), while lions and tigers rarely top 600 pounds (272 kg).

Conversely, if a male tiger and lioness mate, their child exhibits dwarfism (or is smaller than either parent) and is called a tigon. Why does this hybrid get a different name? Because most hybrid names are portmanteaus, or mash-ups, that start with the name of the male species and then add the female species.

As menageries kept experimenting, they crossbred all the *Panthera*, or big cat, species, and it worked! Cross a lion with a leopardess, and you got a lipard. A jaguar with a lioness, a jaglion. A leopard with a tigress, a leoger.

These unexpected hybrids became very popular, moneymaking curiosities, and so they were kept in captivity. But even if they had been released into the wild, imagine the confusion of a liger: Do you hunt at night or during the day, alone or with a pack, in the forest or grassland? Would Dad's family even want you around?

A ZOO OF PORTMANTEAUS: ZORSES, WHOLPHINS & STURDDLEFISH, OH MY!

For centuries, people have created hybrids in captivity by allowing different species to mate, either on purpose or by accident. No gene editing required! Mules—the hybrid children of male donkeys and female horses—have been with us since ancient times, and the what-if wonder of strange pairings has led to an entire zoo's worth of experiments. Here are a few more:

- zebra + horse = zorse
- zebra + donkey = zonkey
- camel + llama = cama
- llama + alpaca = huarizo
- goat + sheep = geep
- cow + bison = beefalo
- false killer whale + bottlenose dolphin = wholphin

And hundreds of others without cute names, like hybrid kangaroos and wallabies, jackals and dogs, wild boars and pigs, and more.

Zorses are the hybrid offspring of horses and zebras. This individual has the stripes and short mane of a zebra, but the dark brown coloration of a horse.

One of the world's most incredible and unlikely hybrids, however, was an unexpected accident of genetic engineering. In 2019 Hungarian researchers were trying to breed endangered sturgeon in captivity using gynogenesis, a method of asexual reproduction using the sperm (but not the DNA) from equally endangered paddlefish. Then one day the paddlefish sperm directly fertilized some sturgeon eggs, and more than one hundred hybrid "sturddlefish" were born.

"We never wanted to play around with hybridization," one researcher said. Indeed, as people had once thought about the liger, researchers assumed this was impossible. Sturgeon and paddlefish are both giant freshwater fish, but both species are so old they are considered "living fossils." They are separated by 184 million years of evolution, live on opposite sides of the planet, and have comically mismatched physiques: paddlefish have cricket-bat snouts and eat plankton, while sturgeon are tough-hided carnivores.

Oh well. Researchers plan to keep the sturddlefish in captivity, without making more. They don't want to release them into the wild because, if sturddlefish mated with either parent species, which remain critically endangered, the hybrids could mess up their genetics.

While scientists assume these sturddlefish are sterile, they also know they might not be. And as it happens, they know this because of modern research into the liger, which has opened our eyes to a strange truth about hybrids that's changed our understanding of species, evolution, and ourselves.

HYBRIDS & EVOLUTION

Until Charles Darwin proposed the theory of evolution in his 1859 book *On the Origin of Species,* scientists believed animal species were fixed and unchanging. Born a tiger, always a tiger. (That said, even before Darwin, scientists recognized that plant species are not fixed and unchanging, but plants are a different story.)

People knew that different animal species could mate and produce hybrid offspring, but those hybrids, such as mules, were almost always sterile, which meant that the hybrids couldn't reproduce. This seemed to prove an abiding rule: in nature, different animal species weren't supposed to mix. Animal hybrids were fascinating failures, evolutionary dead ends, and at first, all the *Panthera* hybrids seemed sterile.

The thinking went, If lions and tigers could breed fertile children, wouldn't the world already be full of ligers? Even today, none have been seen in the wild.

Then, in the 1979, the Alipore Zoo in India mated a female tigon with a male lion, and they conceived a cub, a litigon named Cubanacan. This mating led us to realize that only male ligers and tigons are sterile. Female hybrids are fertile, and a lion and a ligress make a liliger.

The Alipore Zoo bred four more litigons, and in 2017 two more litigons were born in China.

This has prompted scientists to study the DNA of all five *Panthera* species much more closely. They have discovered that at some point in their long evolution into different species, all the big cats have crossbred with one another. They know this because some of those hybrids were fertile, mated again with their parent species, and left telltale snippets of DNA in the surviving species. For instance, the jaguar's optic nerve contains two lion genes, which means a fertile jaglion once existed in the wild.

This is called introgressive hybridization, or introgression, and genome studies are discovering that introgression is "prolific," not rare. Far from being dead ends or monstrosities, hybrids are a natural part of evolution.

"Increasingly," one study found, "evidence is being uncovered to show how profoundly hybridization has influenced the natural evolution of taxa as diverse as butterflies, sharks, finches, parrots, dolphins, bears, wolves, old world primates, or even modern humans."

That's right, us.

Sixty thousand years ago, when ancestral humans left Africa, they met two other human species: Neanderthals in Europe and Denisovans in Asia. These species mated and created hybrids, who mated back with our ancestors and left some genes behind.

Many people—though not all—are hybrids who contain from 2 to 6 percent of either Neanderthal or Denisovan DNA.

IF WE'RE ALL HYBRIDS, WHAT IS A SPECIES?

Should we call ourselves humanderthals? Denisumans?

All this genome research has ignited a crisis in taxonomy, or any system for naming and defining species. We already know that all life exists on a continuum. That's the theory of evolution: species change over time, bit by bit, one into another. However, animals such as whales, snails, and lions are obviously different from one another, and a taxonomy divides life's forms into logical categories.

The trouble is, scientists have never been able to agree on how to define a species, and no definition works in all cases. About thirty different "species concepts" currently exist, each with its own approach.

For mammals, the most common is the "biological species concept." According to biologist Edward O. Wilson, a species is a population "capable of freely interbreeding with one another under natural conditions. In short, a species is a closed gene pool that perpetuates itself *in nature.*"

So, if two animals breed in the wild and have fertile offspring, they are the same or similar species. If two animals only breed in captivity and create infertile hybrids, they are different species.

That would make lions and tigers separate species, except that ligers don't fit that definition. Nor do humanderthals . . . and many others.

To explain evolution, scientists have replaced the "tree of life" analogy with the "web of life"—since species aren't unattached branches but rather strands that connect in multiple ways to other strands. Animals are not like atoms in the periodic table. No fixed species exist. Life's signature traits are fluidity, flexibility, and adaptability.

And genetic engineering is only muddying the waters—especially when making conservation decisions and laws based on species definitions. Because of this, remember that species categories reflect *our* distinctions. People are the ones naming animals. Animals don't care what we call them, how we define them, or who we think belongs together and should be able to mate.

As the nineteenth-century botanist Charles Bessey wrote, "Nature produces individuals and nothing more. Species have been invented in order that we may refer to great numbers of individuals collectively."

Darwin himself called genera "merely artificial combinations made for convenience." Accept that, he wrote, and "we shall at least be freed from the vain search for the undiscovered and undiscoverable essence of the term species."

THE FUTURE OF LIGERS

Once we've made a liger, a mule, or a sturddlefish, another question arises: Should we make more?

The answer depends on the hybrid. Being able to mix and match animals like a child's flip book is amazing and fantastical, and without our curiosity about what is possible, we might never have discovered the liger, the litigon, and the role of hybrids in evolution. But once a hybrid exists, whether by accident or design, we need to consider the animal's welfare and whether, if released into nature, it might negatively affect ecosystems or other species.

When people make hybrids of domestic species, such as mules, zorses, and geeps, they usually keep and care for the hybrids like other farm animals, and so the ethics of animal welfare reflect those of the farm (see part 3) and of companion animals (see part 4). Scientists also

This liliger cub is the offspring of a male lion and a female liger.

make hybrids to serve human medicine (see part 5) and for research. But researchers don't need more ligers. We've already learned *Panthera*'s genetic secrets.

Occasionally, conservationists make wild hybrids to improve troubled ecosystems (see part 2) and to help save an existing, critically endangered species—which has been tried with the Florida panther and certain rhinos (see chapter 3). Otherwise, wild hybrids are often considered threats to existing species and ecosystems, not unlike invasive species. As with sturddlefish, even if ligers could survive in nature and reproduce on their own, conservationists don't want to risk them mating with their endangered parent species, whose genetics might become permanently altered, triggering who knows what other impacts.

This means the only future for modern ligers is a life in captivity. So when deciding whether to make more, the animal welfare ethics we need to consider are those of zoos.

One purpose zoos serve is to support wildlife conservation by breeding and increasing the populations of endangered species. While conservationists debate the usefulness of zoo breeding programs, this doesn't apply to the liger, an animal no one is trying to "conserve."

Otherwise, zoos are primarily a form of education and entertainment, and as in the past, zoos find that ligers are very profitable attractions. They draw visitors and make money. People are understandably fascinated by these epic beings. Who doesn't want to see Hercules, a male liger kept at a South Carolina park, who has been dubbed the "largest living cat" by the *Guinness World Records* and clocks in at 922 pounds (418 kg)?

Yet captivity is difficult for ligers (and for many large, intelligent, social mammals, including elephants, great apes, and rhinos). Ligers are not always born healthy. Many captive-bred, hybrid big cats (such as white tigers) can suffer from genetic problems due to inbreeding, and due to their enormity, ligers can suffer physical ailments like arthritis. Captivity can also cause depression.

So who would benefit from creating more ligers? It seems mainly humans and mostly for our own enjoyment.

About a hundred ligers currently exist, and in the 2004 film *Napoleon Dynamite*, Napoleon says the liger is "my favorite animal . . . bred for its skills in magic."

Unfortunately, one reason we know that isn't true is because, if ligers really did possess magic, it's doubtful any would choose a painful life in a cage.

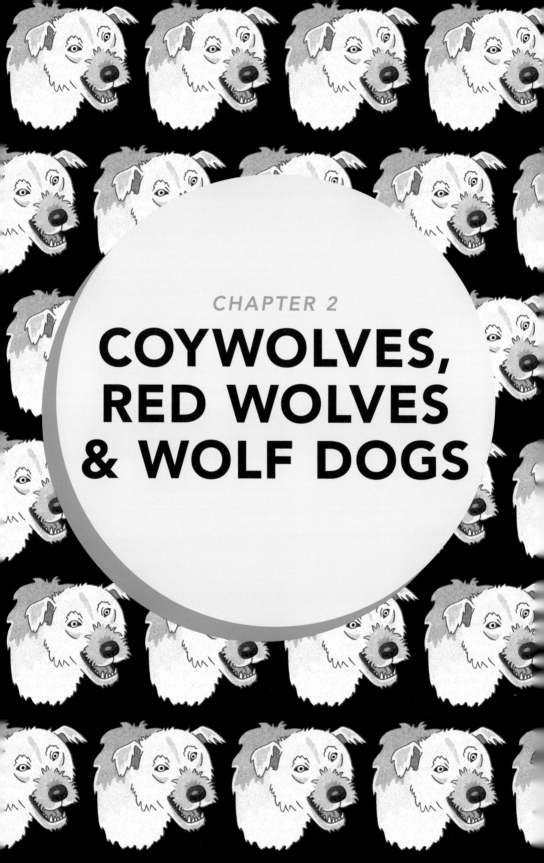

CHAPTER 2
COYWOLVES, RED WOLVES & WOLF DOGS

Wolves, by turning into dogs, were humanity's first lesson in genetic engineering—they were the original magic trick. They taught us that animals *can* change and that through selective breeding we can modify animals till they possess the traits we want.

Wolves, dogs, and coyotes seem to be teaching us another lesson about biological change: it's impossible to stop.

Because of us—because of hunting, the impacts of cities and industry, vanishing wilderness, the declines and extinctions of species, and other environmental harm—many wild species are changing, and evolving, even when we don't want them to.

THE CONFUSING LIVES OF CANIDS

Wolves, coyotes, and dogs belong to the Canidae family. After humans, canids are the most adaptable and widespread land mammal on Earth. We love domestic dogs as our "best friend," but we're much less fond of wild canids because of their skills as top predators. Throughout history, people have often tried to exterminate wolves and coyotes, sometimes successfully.

What we've learned from these efforts is that removing top predators from wild landscapes can undermine entire ecosystems. A negative domino effect can follow a top predator's disappearance. Prey species such as deer can become overpopulated, which can affect plants, which in turn affects every species that depends on those plants, and so on.

In conservation, bringing back top predators is an important part of healing damaged environments. Conservationists have successfully restored habitats in Yellowstone National Park in part by reintroducing gray wolves to the region. Conservationists also want to save endangered species for the sake of the animals themselves—even wolves, who can be hard to live with. Conservationists are dedicated to the belief that no species deserves to become extinct because of us.

But wolves and other canids are making this difficult. Apparently, canids never got the memo that they are no longer supposed to change.

For instance, in North America, eastern wolves, coyotes, and feral dogs have intermixed in the wild to create a new hybrid: the coywolf. This medium-sized canid mutt is an almost ideal predator for our human-dominated world. The coywolf has the wolf's pack-hunting instincts and enough bulk to hunt deer, which coyotes can't do. But like coyotes, coywolves are comfortable living near humanity's hubbub.

Similarly, packs of wild wolf dogs have become a problem in Europe. This wild hybrid is so successful it "threatens the 'genetic identity' of wolves," according to one report. If these wolf dogs were to mate with Europe's remaining gray wolves, those gray wolves would

Wolf dog hybrids exist in the wild and are also kept as pets. However, canine-wolf hybrids that are too "wild" can be unsuitable domestic companions for the home.

become "extinct" as a genetically unique species. This is exactly what conservationists fear might happen if ligers and sturddlefish were turned loose in the landscape.

But people don't seem to mind wolf dogs if they live in our yards. There may be as many or more captive wolf dogs as there are wild wolves left in nature—around 250,000 or less.

And researchers think some gray wolves may again be evolving in a process similar to domestication. Living near people is changing their behavior, which is changing their bodies and turning them into not another type of friendly dog but a wild predator better suited to modern life.

Is that OK? Since species adapt and change, should we shrug and say that's evolution? Should we celebrate and shout: *Hurray, the wolf is dead! Long live coywolves, wolf dogs, or whatever it is canids are turning into!*

Maybe. But almost by definition that isn't the goal of conservation. When it comes to saving endangered species, hybrids are a problem conservationists try to stop.

WHEN IS A WOLF NO LONGER A WOLF?
Consider the red wolf.

From the moment North America's European settlers arrived, they relentlessly exterminated wolves till America was virtually wolf-free (Alaska and Canada aside). By the 1970s, the red wolf—once the Southeast's dominant predator—was reduced to a few scraggly packs in Texas and Louisiana, and these last individuals were mating with coyotes. Normally, wolves and coyotes are competitors, but red wolves lacked enough suitable mates. That is another lesson we're learning: when the only way to survive is to reproduce with distant relatives, animals will.

To save the critically endangered red wolf—and also to restore balance to Southeast ecosystems—conservationists devised a radical

Red wolves range from 55 to 85 pounds (25 to 39 kg), which is smaller than gray wolves and twice as large as coyotes. But similar to coyotes, red wolves have long, lanky legs and black-speckled reddish fur.

plan: capture all the remaining red wolves, weed out the hybrids, breed the wolves in captivity, and then release them back into their original territory. Hopefully, this would protect the red wolf's genes and rebuild a self-sustaining population.

One issue with this plan is that scientists have never been able to agree on what exactly a red wolf is. Some say it is a hybrid (perhaps created only a few thousand years ago). All red wolves share some coyote genes (and coyotes are 20 percent wolf), and red wolves look like modern coywolves: medium build, rusty-auburn fur. Others insist that, although they are closely related, the red wolf diverged from coyotes about 150,000 years ago, making it a distinct species.

The difference matters. If the red wolf is classified as a "hybrid," it doesn't qualify for protection under the Endangered Species Act. And if it isn't protected, it will disappear: either hunted by us or absorbed into a genetic "hybrid swarm" with coyotes.

In 1973 the US Fish and Wildlife Service determined that the red wolf is a unique species that deserves protection, and by 1987, the Red Wolf Recovery Program began releasing captive-bred red wolves into North Carolina. This success—adding wolves, not subtracting them—was rightly celebrated as a conservation miracle.

Then it happened again. Coyotes that had migrated into North Carolina to escape human persecution in the West started mating with red wolves and creating more coywolves.

Conservationists returned to work: they drove coyotes away from the red wolf's territory, killed any coywolf hybrids, and used DNA tracking to monitor and manage red wolves with genetic precision. The wild red wolf population increased—reaching over a hundred—but it has never become self-sustaining. By 2020 researchers estimated that only ten to twenty red wolves still lived in the wild, even as more red wolf–coyote hybrids were discovered in Galveston, Texas.

This Galveston population caused one biologist to wonder: "What protection, or any, should be implemented for an animal that is 50 percent super-endangered species and 50 percent coyote?"

According to current conservation laws, none.

THE EVOLUTION OF CONSERVATION

In conservation, letting endangered species go extinct without a fight is considered wrong, especially when people are the main reason a species is endangered. But from a conservation standpoint, letting red wolves disappear into canid soup is also wrong, since the result is the same: no more red wolves. By and large, conservation's central goal is to preserve wilderness and wild species as they are—or ideally to restore them to the way they were *before* human impacts and meddling.

For instance, if people released ligers into the wild and they started creating a "hybrid swarm," this might result in a world with more ligers than wild lions or tigers. This is easy to prevent: just keep any existing ligers in captivity. But if red wolves and coyotes interbreed in nature on their own, then the only way to preserve red wolves as a species is to interfere and manage their wild populations. This is what we've been doing, and we can't do it forever. It's too expensive. And it's another definition of failure.

Conservation *success* is when species and habitats recover in self-sustaining ways that no longer require human caretaking. This is why, according to evolutionary biologist Chris Thomas, conservation itself may need to evolve. Restoring nature to what it was before humans is becoming increasingly impossible. Since we now know that species evolve in part by forming hybrids, "the idea that humans can or should police hybridization is ludicrous," Thomas writes.

He also believes that conservation should look forward, not back. If endangered species transform before our eyes—say, if red wolves themselves choose to mate with coyotes and become more successful

Adult coyotes range from 20 to 45 pounds (9 to 20 kg). They have adapted well to modern, human-impacted environments and can even thrive in cities.

coywolves—we should accept this new animal, embrace this wild hybrid, and change our laws to protect them and their habitats so they can thrive.

This idea is bittersweet, since it can mean accepting the loss of familiar, even beloved species. But Thomas is an optimist. "Given how much and how fast humans have changed the world," he writes, "it is entirely credible that we are now living through the most rapid period of evolution since the aftermath of the extinction of the dinosaurs 66 million years ago."

Human impacts have certainly sparked an extinction crisis, but is this also a revolution of evolution? Wild canids are an example of how nature can recalibrate to sustain itself. As chapter 4 explores further, interbreeding is one way for animals to change rapidly in a rapidly changing world.

CHAPTER 3

RHINOS: BLACK, WHITE & GRAY

Only two northern white rhinos exist—a mother and daughter, Najin and Fatu—and they have been called the walking dead. When they die, their species will be extinct.

Just a handful of other times have we known the last living member of a species: Martha, the last passenger pigeon, died on September 1, 1914. Lonesome George, the last Pinta Island giant tortoise, died on June 24, 2012.

We will also remember Najin and Fatu. Rhinos are leathery, prehistoric tanks with sloping foreheads, long eyelashes, and absurd horns sprouting from adorable, wide snouts. They have no natural predators besides humans, and if we didn't hunt them, they would survive unbothered, as they have for over fifty million years.

But northern white rhinos don't have to go extinct. Not if we can make more of them.

Najin (*left*) and Fatu, a mother and daughter, are the last two remaining northern white rhinos. Both are protected from poachers by armed guards in the Ol Pejeta Conservancy in Kenya.

Conservation is often treated like a numbers game. Success is often measured by counting. If we increase the population of an endangered species so that it is healthy and self-sustaining, that's success! The species will no longer be "endangered," and if we continue to protect their habitat, the animals will no longer need our help.

But making more northern white rhinos would seem impossible. There are only two, and both are female. But as conservation biologist Phil Seddon has said, "The new genetic engineering technologies . . . change everything."

SOUTHERN WHITE RHINOS: BACK FROM THE BRINK

Other rhino species have already gone extinct, and of the five remaining species, four are endangered or threatened. Three live in Asia—the Javan, Sumatran, and Indian rhinos. Two live in Africa— black rhinos and white rhinos, which have two subspecies, southern and northern.

Despite their names, all rhinos are gray—like sheet metal or storm clouds. Species differ by shape, behavior, habitat, and horns. Some have two horns (black, Sumatran); others, one (white, Indian, Javan).

The only rhino species that isn't in trouble is the southern white rhino, though it too was once declared extinct. Its astounding recovery is one of conservation's greatest success stories.

By the late nineteenth century, people assumed the southern white rhino was gone. For decades, big-game hunters had shot this rhino as a prize, and they kept shooting until they couldn't find any more. Then a dozen rhinos were unexpectedly discovered in South Africa. In 1897, rather than shoot them, people established the Umfolozi Game Reserve to protect them. This worked so well that by the 1950s the southern white rhino population had increased to more than four hundred, beyond what the park could hold. So an Umfolozi ranger, Ian Player, single-handedly led the relocation of southern white rhinos around the world and back into some of their original range. By 2020 about eighteen thousand white rhinos were tending to their ancient business within a variety of protected parks and preserves.

This epitomizes how simple conservation can be: if endangered species have enough space, healthy ecosystems, and minimal human interference, they can take care of themselves. Indeed, the current extinction crisis could be thought of as a coexistence crisis. Endangered species need humans to be better neighbors, and traditional conservation focuses on protecting habitats and regulating people so animals can rebuild their populations on their own.

As in the past, the main threat for rhinos is poaching, and the prize is the horn. Since poachers don't care about park boundaries, the challenge for conservationists is to halt the obsession with rhino horn. This might stem the epidemic of poaching. Until then, even southern white rhinos won't remain entirely safe.

THE LAST STAND: CROSSBREEDING, STEM CELLS, AND CLONING

To save the remaining endangered rhino species, conservationists are trying to help them reproduce by using every gadget in the gene-editing tool kit. They've tried captive breeding programs—like the red wolf program—but rhinos don't breed well in captivity, and they breed slowly. When populations get extremely low, inbreeding becomes an issue, since inbred populations are prone to genetic and health problems. Restoring a critically endangered species also means boosting its genetic diversity.

To improve genetic diversity, one method is crossbreeding. Technically, this changes the animal's genetics and creates a hybrid (such as a coywolf or liger). So conservationists only use it as a last resort. Typically, they crossbreed only closely related subspecies to minimize any physical, behavioral, and genetic differences in the new animal.

Crossbreeding saved the endangered Florida panther. The species had been hunted down to about thirty mostly inbred males (that struggled to reproduce). Conservationists relocated eight female Texas pumas to the region, and this worked. The subspecies mated, and a new, healthier panther population bloomed, which currently numbers over a hundred.

In 2014 conservationists tried to crossbreed Najin and Fatu with a male southern white rhino, but they discovered that neither female can carry a baby to term.

The current approach is in vitro fertilization. Since 2019 eggs have periodically been taken from Najin and Fatu. As of 2021, five eggs had been successfully fertilized with sperm taken (and frozen) years ago from Suni, one of the last male northern white rhinos. These viable embryos have themselves been put on ice until they can be transferred into southern white rhino surrogate mothers. Scientists hope these surrogate mothers can bring the embryos to term and give birth to northern white rhino babies.

Conservationists are also considering another method: cloning. They know it can work because they've already done it.

In 2019 the black-footed ferret became the first endangered species native to North America to be cloned (using the methods described in chapter 9). Black-footed ferret numbers once dwindled to eighteen. Through a captive breeding program, conservationists successfully increased their numbers, but with one problem: all the new black-footed ferrets were essentially half siblings. They lacked enough genetic diversity to create a healthy, self-sustaining population. So scientists are creating clones from the frozen tissue of unrelated black-footed ferrets (who lived in the 1980s!), then using those clones in the captive breeding program. Ultimately, the children (and grandchildren) of those clones will be released into the wild.

The ferret tissue samples came from the subzero cryobank at the San Diego Frozen Zoo. That cryobank also has preserved frozen

There are around 18,000 southern white rhinos living in Africa—mostly in protected areas and game reserves. They are the only rhino species that is not endangered.

cells and tissue from a dozen northern white rhinos (both males and females). Between them, these cells can provide enough genetic material to restore a healthy northern white rhino population.

Of course, it's possible that, before any of this happens, Najin and Fatu will die.

EGGS AND OMELETS: MEASURING SUCCESS

Just because we can clone northern white rhinos, *should* we?

If saving this species involved only a numbers game—creating more rhinos—that's straightforward. Cloning and in vitro fertilization are expensive and difficult, but they will do the job. Afterward, if we lock northern white rhinos away in zoos and enclosures, where poachers can't get them, some will always exist somewhere.

But the truth is, conservation is about more than numbers, which are only one measure of success. If a species exists only in captivity, conservationists call it "functionally extinct" or "extinct in the wild," no matter how many there are. The animals are not gone from the world, but they are, in effect, gone from nature. The goal of wildlife preservation is not to fill up our zoos. Conservationists seek to preserve and restore healthy, biodiverse, self-sustaining ecosystems that don't need human caretaking. Even if scientists use genetic engineering to save a specific endangered species, the ultimate measure of success is establishing wild populations within functioning habitats.

Further, living in captivity changes animals. For example, more tigers live in cages (perhaps twelve thousand) than in the wild (maybe four thousand). Not only do tiger subspecies tend to crossbreed in captivity—creating a genetic muddle that blurs subspecies distinctions—but nothing about everyday life is the same. In captivity, tigers experience stress, have limited movement, can't hunt, are fed what we give them, interact with other tigers in different ways, and can develop an unhealthy familiarity with humans—all of which can eventually make the animals unfit to fend for themselves in nature.

Thus, even if people engineer hundreds more northern white rhinos, the species will still be considered "functionally extinct" if the animals remain in captivity and play no role in a natural ecosystem.

Healthy ecosystems need all their pieces, but certain species—such as wolves, tigers, rhinos, and more—play unique and even irreplaceable roles. When too many species disappear, and as ecosystems fall apart, biologist Edward O. Wilson warns, "to reassemble them would be like unscrambling an egg."

This is why conservationists try so hard to preserve endangered species as they are and to change them as little as possible. Of course, genetic engineering can make more eggs and more animals, but only nature really knows how everything goes together to make an omelet.

CHAPTER 4

PIZZLIES & NARLUGAS

n 2006 a hunter shot what he thought was a polar bear in the Northwest Territories of Canada. Then he looked closer and got worried. Despite its vanilla ice-cream fur, the animal had several grizzly bear traits: brown patches, long claws, and a hunched back. If he'd killed a grizzly, which was restricted under local laws, the hunter could have been fined or even jailed.

When the DNA test came back, he breathed a sigh of relief. He hadn't shot a grizzly *or* a polar bear. He'd killed a pizzly, the first polar bear–grizzly hybrid ever documented in the wild.

CLIMATE CHANGE HYBRIDS

At least eight more wild pizzlies have since been found (thankfully, not all killed). Pizzlies also occur occasionally in captivity. Like *Panthera* species, we know these bears have experienced introgression, or fertile

Due to climate change, polar bears and grizzly bears are increasingly sharing territory and mating, creating wild hybrid pizzlies and grolar bears (the name differs depending on which parent species is male).

crossbreeding, even after they evolved into separate species (which different genome studies say happened anywhere from 400,000 to 4 million years ago).

The question these wild sightings raise is: We know polar bears and grizzlies can and will mate with each other on their own, so why are they mating together now?

Maybe . . . *the weather*?

That's what scientists believe. The steady melting of polar ice due to global warming is forcing polar bears to spend more time on land and extending the grizzly's territory farther north. When these two species share habitat, they normally fight, but sometimes they mate, and warmer weather is bringing them together more often.

And more climate change hybrids are popping up all over the world.

Narlugas, hybrids of narwhals and beluga whales, are another example. Narwhals have no teeth, and belugas have no tusk, so the narluga's genes split the difference: they are tuskless, with a mangled set of teeth at all angles, some spiraling as if they were a tusk.

Since it's easier for marine habitats to overlap as waters warm, marine animals seem to be crossbreeding more often. Hybrids have been observed among blacktip shark species, between bowhead and right whales, and among blue whales, minke whales, various seals, and harbor and Dall's porpoises.

This remixing is forcing us to rethink the role of hybrids in evolution. The old view—that wild hybrids are infertile, unhelpful evolutionary mistakes—doesn't fit the evidence. As evolutionary biologist Chris Thomas says, "Speciation by hybridization is likely to be a signature of the Anthropocene."

That is because, when species interbreed and have fertile children, those hybrids can sometimes be *more* successful than either parent species. Hybrid children gain new genes and new traits, and if those changes improve survival, they can get passed along much faster than genes could ever change on their own to develop similar traits.

A narwhal's long, spiral tusk—which can be up to ten feet (3 m) long—is actually an enormous tooth. Maybe that's why, in hybrid narlugas, the teeth can emerge spiraled, as if mimicking a tusk.

In particular, when polar bears mate with grizzlies, their pizzly children may be acquiring some useful grizzly traits that will help them survive in warmer, ice-free environments.

Scientists are discovering that when ecosystems and climates are stable, species tend to be stable. But when environments undergo extreme, rapid upheaval—as in the climate crisis—species change as fast as they possibly can.

This leads to another conservation question: Should humans help species change even faster?

FROM DEFENSE TO OFFENSE: ENGINEERING EVOLUTION

One striking lesson from all these stories is how fast evolution can occur when environments change, as well as how fatal it is when evolution moves too slowly.

Wolves are adapting by forming new canid hybrids that seem better suited to changes in their habitats, but what about rhinos? To save themselves from human poaching, rhinos would have to get rid of their horns. Or rather, evolve to be hornless. In theory, that's not impossible.

Over the last forty years, a similar adaption has occurred among African elephants in Mozambique's Gorongosa National Park. Some African elephants are born naturally tuskless, and after a period of intense poaching in Mozambique from 1977 to 1992, the elephants who survived tended not to have tusks. This meant the genetic instructions for tusklessness were passed on more frequently to the next generation, which has made tusklessness common among these elephants. Of course, the animals didn't decide to change to avoid poaching, but that's the beauty of evolution: genetic inheritance fosters the physical traits that lead to survival.

Unfortunately, modern rhinos aren't known to be naturally hornless, so this doesn't seem to be a genetic trait they already possess. Nor do rhinos have a hornless cousin they might mate with, similar to how narwhals can crossbreed with belugas to create hornless narlugas.

However, one visit to our gene-editing workshop, and it could be *snip, snip*—here's your revised hornless self! If rhinos had no horn to steal, poachers *might* leave them alone. If some genetic researcher discovered the right genes to snip, should they do it?

Our new genetic tools leapfrog evolution, and some scientists think we should use them not just for reproduction—to increase populations of endangered species—but to alter troubled species to improve their chances of survival.

"The thing is," says geneticist George Church, "we can artificially create wild species that are better adapted to a world affected and modified by human beings. We can make them more resistant to lead, more resistant to pesticides, more heat- or drought-resistant."

Many species face environmental threats. For instance, populations of frogs, bats, and bees are being decimated by illnesses and viruses.

One suggestion is to engineer disease resistance in those animals. Or we could engineer pests and invasive species to commit genetic suicide so they don't destroy natural habitats (for more on this, see chapter 17).

Here's another problem the pizzly embodies: when climates change, species often save themselves by migrating. They move to more suitable habitat. But human civilization often blocks animals from doing this, leaving species with no other place to go. In many cases, if species can't adapt to where they currently live, they might go extinct.

As de-extinction advocate Stewart Brand says, genetic engineering is "emblematic of the current change in the approach to protecting species. We're going from defense to offense. We're taking action—trying stuff, experimenting, not just trying to conserve the little that's left using old methods."

CARETAKERS OF NATURE, TENDING GARDENS OF WILDERNESS

Deliberately engineering wild species to improve them has been called "directed," "prescriptive," or "guided" evolution. As Chris Thomas asks, "Why should we not aspire to a world where it is as legitimate to facilitate new gains as it is to avoid losses?"

Conservation already tinkers with nature. It influences evolution by choosing which species to save and which habitats to protect and restore. Since all species change to survive, why not genetically hurry some species along in their evolutionary journeys?

There are a few reasons to be cautious.

First, many say that instead of changing animals, people need to change. If we tried to be better neighbors—by not hunting endangered species, polluting, turning wilderness into suburbs, and clearing rain forests for farms—this might be the best way to help nature and all species survive climate change.

Another reason is that if we tinker with species, those changes are forever. And if we make a mistake, we could make animals less fit or even enhance them *too well* so they become pests or threats to other species.

Like many of the issues discussed in this book, this isn't necessarily an either-or question. When it comes to conservation, the most effective solutions might require a both/and approach. We should preserve natural habitat and write laws that regulate human behavior to protect endangered species—the approach of traditional conservation—while using genetic engineering when that provides the best (or maybe only) way to save animals and improve ecosystems.

We can't escape becoming caretakers of nature. We already are, but all this tinkering makes people wonder: Is wilderness still "wilderness" if we manage it like a garden? Would a rhino still be a rhino if we genetically altered it?

George Church replies: "This technology doesn't change species in essence; it just makes them better adapted to today's environment. That's just like all the mutations that have enabled people to adapt to urban life over the last few millennia. They haven't stopped us being human."

Hold that thought as we explore the other ways people are tinkering with species.

HOW WE GOT HERE: A GENETIC ENGINEERING TIMELINE

32,000–14,000 BCE: The first domesticated species appears. With human help, the wolf evolves into the dog.

11,000–2,500 BCE: People domesticate sheep, goats, pigs, cows, cats, horses, camels, and other animals, along with wheat, rice, corn, beans, potatoes, apples, and other crops.

CE 1856–1863: Austrian monk Gregor Mendel experiments with pea plants and discovers rules of heredity that become the foundation of modern genetics.

1859: Charles Darwin publishes *On the Origin of Species*, which proposes the theory of evolution.

1909: Danish botanist Wilhelm Johannsen coins the term *gene*, naming the mechanism controlling inherited traits. He is inspired by the Greek word *gonos*, for offspring; only later does *gene* come to refer to a sequence of DNA.

1910–1915: American biologist Thomas Hunt Morgan experiments with fruit flies. His research leads to chromosome maps. These explain the mechanism of heredity and natural selection.

1940s: DNA is shown to be the heredity material.

1952: Scientists transfer an embryo nucleus into a frog egg to create the first cloned animal, a tadpole.

1953: On April 25, James Watson and Francis Crick publish a paper on the double-helix structure of DNA based on their, Maurice Wilkins's, and Rosalind Franklin's research. This day is known as DNA Day.

1971–1972: The first gene-splicing experiments include Stanley Cohen and Herbert Boyer inserting frog genes into *E. coli* bacteria, creating recombinant DNA. These discoveries launch the biotech industry.

1980: The first transgenic mice are produced.

1983: The first genetically modified (GM) plant is tobacco, followed in the 1990s with modified varieties of potatoes, tomatoes, corn, and others. Most changes are to protect against pests.

1987: A transgenic mouse is developed that produces beneficial human proteins in its milk. This technique revolutionizes drug manufacturing.

1992: The first glowing organism, a transgenic version of *E. coli*, is created using green fluorescent proteins (GFP). This discovery revolutionizes genetic research.

1996: On July 5, Dolly the sheep, the first animal clone made from the cells of an adult animal, is born.

1998: A microscopic nematode worm is the first multicellular organism to have its entire genome sequenced.

2003: The Human Genome Project, after thirteen years and a cost of $3 billion, announces the first complete sequencing of an entire human genome.

    Using cryopreserved cells, the first extinct species is cloned, a Pyrenean ibex, or bucardo. The newborn dies minutes later.

2005: A South Korean lab clones the first dog, Snuppy, and the first wolf.

2010: J. Craig Venter unveils Synthia, the world's first synthetic life-form, a living modified bacterial organism containing portions of synthetic DNA created letter by letter.

2012: Jennifer Doudna and Emmanuelle Charpentier develop the CRISPR-Cas9 gene-editing technique, a cheaper, more precise tool that revolutionizes gene editing.

2018: Chinese scientist He Jiankui announces the birth of the first genetically modified humans, twin girls whose embryos were edited with CRISPR to be immune to HIV.

2021: The first genetically modified animal approved by the US Food & Drug Administration (FDA) for human consumption, the AquAdvantage salmon, is sold to and served in US restaurants.

2025–2030: This is the target completion date for the chickenosaurus and the de-extinct passenger pigeon.

PART 2

BRINGING BACK THE DEAD

Using the tools of genetic engineering, we are bringing back the dead. One day, you could have the pleasure of meeting a woolly mammoth, a passenger pigeon, or even a dinosaur.

Why resurrect extinct species? Most often, de-extinction is pursued for the same reasons that drive wildlife conservation: to repair and heal the natural world. Sometimes, no living species can perform the same role in the ecosystem as an extinct species, so scientists are trying to revive those long-gone animals.

This raises a few *teeny-tiny* questions:

Does this mean extinction no longer exists and doesn't matter? (No.)

Won't most "unextinct species" really be *new* animals? (Yes.)

Couldn't unleashing long-dead creatures create havoc, even disaster? (Um, well . . . *maybe*.)

De-extinction is definitely coming, though, so we'll find out soon. As evolutionary biologist Beth Shapiro writes, "What is the point, after all, of bringing a species back from the dead if it is not to reestablish a wild population?"

CHAPTER 5

CHICKENOSAURUS

Let's get one thing straight: Jack Horner doesn't want to build *Jurassic Park*.

He *is* trying to make a dinosaur, but if it ever hatches, it will be the size of a chicken. Why? Because, genetically, it will be a chicken—one that's been manipulated to grow a dinosaur-like tail, snout, teeth, and forelimbs with claws instead of wings.

He calls this proposed creature *chickenosaurus*, and it's this kind of insane scientific project that makes a goofball, about-to-die, secondary character want to shout: *Didn't you see the movie? Don't you know what happens when you resurrect the fiercest predator ever to walk the earth!?*

Yes, Horner knows. He's been the lead scientific consultant on all the *Jurassic Park* films, and he wants to make clear that what happens in the movies can't happen in real life. It's impossible to clone dinosaurs, period. Any intact dinosaur DNA is lost forever. So forget any fantasies (or fears) of dinosaur islands teeming with velociraptors, pterodactyls, and *T. rexes*.

But if he can't resurrect an actual dinosaur, what makes Horner think he can build a new one?

Good question.

REWINDING EVOLUTION

Jack Horner is a paleontologist. He's spent his entire professional life digging up fossils and trying to piece together dinosaurs, but, he confesses, "what we would really love to do, if we could, is bring 'em back alive."

That's impossible, so his current plan is to make a new one—which would be ridiculous except for one thing.

"Dinosaurs never did go extinct," Horner writes. "Birds are dinosaurs, descended from theropod dinosaurs, related to *T. rex*, and with a great library of dinosaur genes in their genome."

Wait—we've been living with dinosaurs all along!?

Theropod dinosaurs, such as the *Tyrannosaurus Rex*, lived during the Jurassic Period about 150 million years ago. Theropods are the ancestors of all birds, including chickens.

Yep. Flocks and flocks of them.

Basically, all scientists agree that modern birds are "avian dinosaurs." Extinct theropods, in particular, share all major physical traits with modern birds, including feathers, except for four: they had teeth, a snout instead of a beak, a long tail, and arms with claws instead of wings.

Horner's goal is nothing less than to "reverse the evolutionary process and get an embryonic chick to develop into a dinosaur instead."

While Horner would love to look a living dinosaur in its beady eye—to know what dinosaurs sounded like and how they behaved—he is really seeking the answer to bigger questions. How did theropods turn into birds in the first place—and how does any species change into another? How did ancient ungulates evolve into both hippos and whales? Or ancient lemurs into humans? The fossil record shows this happened, that all beings evolve from ancient forms, but we still haven't proved *how* this happens on a genetic level.

"The fundamental reason for attempting to rewind evolution is to learn how evolution occurs. Like a teenager with an old car, you take it apart to learn how it works." Horner's reason for making a dinosaur is science's oldest: curiosity about life.

CREATING CHICKENOSAURUS

If all birds are avian dinosaurs, here's another question: Why choose a chicken?

As any home cook will tell you, convenience. Chickens are the most studied bird (theirs was the first avian genome to be mapped), they are cheap and plentiful, and few object to using their eggs or embryos in research.

The mechanism that Horner and other researchers think is the key is epigenetics, or gene expression. As an embryo develops, chemical signals instruct its genes to turn on and off at certain times. These signals guide the genes to express themselves in specific ways to create a specific body, and this process continues throughout life. Yet if those chemical signals are altered—which can happen due to changes in the mother's diet or in the environment—those same genes would express themselves differently, resulting in slightly different physical traits. A different body.

Repeat this over and over, and this is the theory for how one species can evolve into two with virtually the same genes. Since the 1970s, scientists have speculated that, as paleontologist Stephen Jay Gould once said, "Changes in the timing of embryonic development could make dramatic changes in evolution."

Or, Horner says, "On the evolutionary voyage from dinosaur to falcon, what happens is not that a whole new set of falcon genes is developed for beak, wings, and eyes. Instead the instructions for limbs, feathers, eyes, and tail are changed so that the same building blocks of the vertebrate body are put together in different ways."

That is the very definition of tinkering: taking what exists and fiddling with it, changing small parts but not the whole. Evolution makes something a little different with each generation, which is why, Horner says, "all living things are part of a continuum."

By working in reverse—and tinkering with a chicken embryo's genes so they express the ancient form of a dinosaur—Horner hopes to prove this theory.

Chickens may not look like "avian dinosaurs," but scientists hope to reveal the "dinosaur within" by manipulating a chicken embryo to develop arms, claws, a snout, teeth, and a long tail.

Whether he can alter an embryo in these ways, and whether that embryo will hatch into a living, breathing, healthy, dinosaur-like chicken, Horner doesn't know, but he's about halfway along. Researchers have already modified an embryo's beak to become a snout and to grow teeth.

Next, Horner is optimistic that they can turn wings into limbs and claws. "If you follow the development of a chicken embryo closely," he says, "you will see five buds at the end of the developing wing, buds that also appear in the embryos of mice and people. The buds become fingers in a human embryo and claws in a mouse. In a chicken, the five buds on a forelimb will lengthen, shorten, disappear, and be fused to fit into the familiar structure that cries out to us for hot sauce."

The tail, though, is the hardest and maybe most important part. Some prehistoric birds had tails, but no modern birds do. At some point, a bird embryo halts the development of what used to be a tail and turns it into a stump. But if researchers can intervene in the right way at the right moment, they should be able to make the tail grow again.

WHEN DINOSAURS ARE BACK

Since the moment he started, Horner has been asked when he will finish, and he's hopeful that chickenosaurus could roar—or squawk— by 2030, if not sooner.

Not only might this prove the evolutionary theories of what's called "evolutionary developmental biology," or evo-devo for short, but the applications of this research could be profound. For instance, applying lessons about embryo development to humans might help prevent certain spinal-cord birth defects.

This could also be used to alter any bird embryo to express ancient traits. Dino-rrific crows, pigeons, eagles, ostriches, and songbirds? *Why not!* Since the genes themselves remain the same, there aren't any worries about unleashing monsters that might reproduce themselves. If chickenosaurus escaped—and if we can trust Hollywood, *you know it will happen*—and mated with a hen or rooster, the offspring's embryo would develop normally. Without the manipulation of researchers, chickenosaurus's genes would express themselves to make a chicken. And if we were hungry, Horner says, "we could stuff it and roast it. It would taste, as the proverb says, like chicken."

No dinosaur resurrection project is without a few dangers, of course, and Horner admits to two.

One, Horner wonders whether this is "fair to the chicken." For the bird, it certainly sounds upsetting—to emerge from an egg with a dinosaur's body. Horner is quick to say that if the hatched being were malformed or in obvious pain, the creature would be killed. "The experiment would only be successful if the animal were comfortable and well-functioning."

Then, putting aside the welfare of chickenosaurus, the other danger is commercial. Because if you can make *one* chickenosaurus . . .

"We've made all kinds of weird dogs and other creatures," Horner says. "Dinosaurs will be one of our domestic animals, and we'll be able to keep them as pets. If we wanted to, I think we'd be able to raise them for meat as well. I'm sure someone'll make a mint from selling them as pets, but it's not going to be me."

Someone definitely will because *some people* will definitely want one. People won't gather them on "dino-bird island." No, they will keep chickenosaurs at home.

As they say in the movies, *What could go wrong?*

CHAPTER 6

WOOLLY MAMMOTH

magine this: One day, vast herds of woolly mammoth are tromping across the Arctic, yet their ski-slope tusks and mountainous backs are just the largest silhouettes. In addition, a cauldron of wildlife crowds a restored Siberian tundra, one as rich with animals as the Serengeti Plain.

Most important, this awe-inducing spectacle would be helping to fight climate change.

That utopian vision is the inspiration driving the epic attempt to de-extinct the woolly mammoth. If successful, this project would realize the earth-shaking potential of bioengineering wild species.

THE FALL OF THE MAMMOTH AND THE MAMMOTH STEPPE

Researchers don't know exactly why mammoths went extinct, but they suspect two main culprits: the weather and humans.

About 11,700 years ago, the last ice age ended as the climate warmed, which shrank the mammoth's habitat and caused population declines. For hundreds of thousands of years, woolly mammoths had been the dominant megaherbivore across the Northern Hemisphere and had survived similar periods of hotter weather—but not with us around. Cro-Magnons, our human ancestors, hunted mammoths with a passion. As mammoths retreated northward, people followed and finished them off, though it took a while. The woolly mammoth's slow decline ended about four thousand years ago, when the last population winked out on Wrangell Island, Alaska.

Human hunting helped cause a wave of large-animal extinctions: the Irish elk, three species of elephants, the woolly rhino, the cave lion, and more. Like Africa today, Siberia once possessed a vast grassland ecosystem, called the mammoth steppe, that supported seemingly endless herds.

Over time, those Siberian grasslands have mostly been replaced by mossy forests and wetlands, and most of the large animals there

Woolly mammoths thrived for millennia. These megaherbivores could reach thirteen feet (4 m) and weigh six tons (5.4 t), and their enormous impact is what created the mammoth steppe in the Arctic.

have disappeared. As the climate warms again, the Arctic's frozen, carbon-rich permafrost soil has begun melting, and this is releasing that stored carbon into the atmosphere. Carbon is a major greenhouse gas. Some estimate that the permafrost contains twice as much carbon as exists in our current atmosphere, and if *all* of it were released, it would be like burning all Earth's remaining forests two and a half times.

To keep that carbon in the ground, the permafrost has to remain frozen. The most effective way to do that, some researchers believe, is to restore those epic herds of grazing animals, including the woolly mammoth.

Undisturbed snow insulates the ground like a blanket, so in winter the soil actually stays warmer than the air. But millions of mammoth feet and reindeer and bison hooves would punch billions of holes in the snow, destroying this insulation and keeping the ground frozen.

Forests also absorb more sunlight than grasslands, which also contributes to warming. But to shrink forests and increase grasslands, we might need the woolly mammoth—because that's what mammoths did: they knocked down trees, trampled saplings, migrated long distances, and fostered more grasses by dispersing grass seeds in their poop. Their mighty presence is what created the mammoth steppe.

In 1996, to test whether herd animals would impact the permafrost, the father-son team of Sergey and Nikita Zimov created Pleistocene Park, a scientific research station in Siberia. The park's fenced area of 7.7 square miles (20 sq. km) has about 150 animals, including reindeer, moose, bison, musk ox, and others. Sergey Zimov says the "animals have created a noticeable effect. . . . Grasses are now the dominant vegetation at many locations [and] carbon storage in the soil is slowly increasing."

Nikita Zimov adds, "What we've shown with Pleistocene Park is that a steppe landscape full of grazing animals could be a simple, inexpensive solution" to halt the melting permafrost.

The real issues are scale and time. Permafrost occupies a fifth of the landmass of the Northern Hemisphere. To affect that requires more than 150 animals and a single woolly mammoth.

It requires countless herds.

A NEW, IMPROVED, BIGGER, HAIRIER ELEPHANT

Enter scientist George Church and the biosciences company Colossal, which is devoted to de-extinction. They are working together to try to bioengineer the mammoth back to life. The effort began in 2012, when it was initially led by the organization Revive & Restore, whose cofounder, Stewart Brand, promised, "We're bringing back the mammoth to restore the steppe in the Arctic. One or two mammoths is not a success. A hundred thousand mammoths is a success."

That remains the goal with Colossal, which was founded in 2021, but standing in the way is a long list of enormous obstacles.

The first is that resurrecting a genuine woolly mammoth is impossible. Evolutionary biologist Beth Shapiro says bluntly, "We will never create an identical clone of a mammoth." That's because cloning requires a preserved *living* cell, and none exist for extinct species like mammoth (or dinosaurs). A cell's DNA starts degrading immediately after death, making it useless for cloning, which is why it's often said, "You can't clone from bone."

However, there's another way: Shapiro and others have painstakingly recovered bits of mammoth DNA from fossils and preserved tissue and sequenced its genome. Using this, Shapiro says, "we can . . . resurrect some of their extinct traits" by inserting bits of mammoth DNA into the genome of the Asian elephant, the mammoth's closest living relative.

Some woolly mammoths, such as this baby mammoth, have been surprisingly well preserved in the Arctic permafrost. These specimens have helped scientists sequence the woolly mammoth's genome, though cloning remains impossible without a living cell.

Rather than make an exact copy, the intention, as Colossal says, is to create "a cold-resistant elephant with all the core biological traits of the woolly mammoth." This animal "will walk like a woolly mammoth, sound like one, [and] be able to inhabit the same ecosystem."

In other words, scientists aren't really de-extincting a prehistoric creature. They are bioengineering a new, transgenic Asian elephant/mammoth (or an elephant with DNA from another species). Perhaps we could call it an elemoth or a woolly Asian mammephant.

Incredibly, the genomes of woolly mammoths and Asian elephants are 99.6 percent similar. Within that 0.4 percent difference, Church and his team are mainly focusing on the mammoth genes that influence three traits: hairy fur, a layer of fat under the skin (for insulation), and blood cells that function at very low temperatures. Then they will copy-and-paste that DNA into living Asian elephant cells using CRISPR-Cas9. CRISPR is like a "programmable molecular scalpel," says Jennifer Doudna, the technique's coinventor. It can find where to cut, slice out genes or a portion of DNA, and then insert or write in new DNA (see figure page 70).

Scientists may also shrink the elephants' ears and insert characteristics from other cold-adapted species such as penguins—traits mammoths never had. "We might be able to do even better than the mammoth did," Church says. "This is about making new species that are better adapted to the modern environment—which is actually much better than making new versions of old ones."

Once they have an edited elephant cell that contains all the changes, the scientists will grow it into an embryo, and this leads to the hardest part: pregnancy. Typically, biologists would insert the embryo into a surrogate female to give birth. The Colossal team might try to use African elephants as surrogate mothers, but implanting embryos is difficult, stressful, and sometimes dangerous for elephants, which are a threatened species.

CRISPR TECHNOLOGY

1

DNA strand

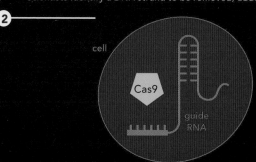

Scientists identify a DNA strand to be removed, added to, or modified.

2

cell

Cas9

guide
RNA

They create guide RNA that has the same genomic code as the DNA being modified. This is combined in a cell with an enzyme called Cas9, which acts like scissors to cut the DNA.

3

The guide RNA finds the matching genomic sequence.

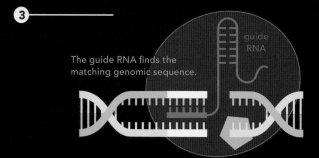

guide
RNA

Then the Cas9 cuts the strand making a break in the DNA helix.

4

healthy DNA strand

Cells are able to detect and repair broken DNA. Once the DNA strand has been added to or modified, enzymes repair it.

An endangered species, Asian elephants live in tropical and subtropical regions in southern Asia. However, some scientists believe that genetically altering Asian elephants to live in colder climates could expand their range and help them survive.

No one wants to harm elephants to make mammoths, so Church hopes to develop an artificial womb. Developing an embryo outside a living womb is called ectogenesis. The concept was pretty much science fiction until 2021, when researchers announced that for the first time, they'd done it: more than one thousand mouse embryos were brought halfway to term in a mechanical womb. Getting the embryos to develop fully is the next challenge, but it's only a matter of time until new reproductive technologies allow us to incubate a brand-new woolly mammoth without needing an actual mother.

CONSERVATION & COEXISTENCE

It could be that de-extincting mammoths won't stop the permafrost from melting, but researchers believe their work may at least help

Asian elephants survive. An endangered species, Asian elephants were modified so they could live in colder places, it would expand their range and increase their numbers. Then, Beth Shapiro says, elephants would "no longer be isolated to pockets of declining habitat in tropical zones of the Old World." This, according to Shapiro, represents the real priority. Not bringing back dead species for their own sake but using genetic engineering "to save species and ecosystems that are alive today from becoming extinct."

This research might also improve human medicine. According to Revive & Restore, "Mammoth hemoglobin . . . may reveal information about mammalian blood useful to treating human diseases, and potentially the future of human space exploration (such as surviving cold environments)."

That's right, bioengineering mammoths could help humans live in space. See why it's so hard to tell science from science fiction anymore?

Still, there is one last obstacle we must overcome for the mammephant to succeed: coexistence. Humans helped drive mammoths to extinction once. Can we stop ourselves from doing it again?

Shapiro says, "Certainly, if we are to make room for extinct species—or for hybrids of extinct and living species—in the real world, we as a society will have to alter our attitudes, our actions, and even our laws. Science is paving the way to resurrect the past. The road, however, will be long, not necessarily direct, and certainly not smooth."

One thing mammephants will need is space. The Arctic has plenty, but people still live there. It's exciting to imagine a landscape filled with trumpeting herds, but their migrations might overrun towns, and if they can knock down forests, no fence will stop them.

Nor are our current wildlife laws written for de-extincted or human-created animals. These beings don't fit any of our definitions of species, so writing regulations will mean, first, defining what they are, and then deciding how to manage and protect them. Technically, a woolly mammephant wouldn't be an "endangered species" because it's never existed before, but we might choose to define and treat them in similar ways. That means deciding whether it's OK to kill them in self-defense (if they threatened to harm people), to eat some as food (so we can grill mammoth steaks again), to hunt them in the wild (once many thousands exist), for tourism companies to conduct "mammephant safaris," for zoos and wildlife parks to display mammephants in captivity, and so on. Coexistence with wild, genetically engineered animals raises lots of new questions and will require new rules.

For mammephants, captivity might be especially cruel. Elephants suffer when they are isolated in zoos because they are among Earth's most intelligent, self-aware, and social mammals. As a close relative, the woolly mammoth might have been equally smart and self-aware, and mammephants will be mostly elephant.

Ultimately, these new animals will have no history, no established society, and no evolved role. When we birth new beings, we also birth a new consciousness. Like us and all animals, woolly mammephants will have minds, emotions, and an urge to survive. No one truly knows, once they are loose in the world, exactly what that urge will lead them to do.

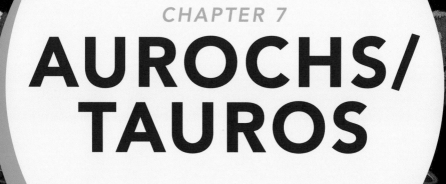

CHAPTER 7

AUROCHS/ TAUROS

fter the wolf, perhaps the most dangerous species we ever domesticated was the aurochs. We have no idea how people did it, but it must have taken guts.

Aurochs suffered no predators. A minivan of muscle, they stood more than 6 feet tall (1.8 m) at the shoulders, and their massive head sprouted two forward-curving, dark-tipped, swordlike, 3-foot-long (0.9 m) horns. Wolves could kill one occasionally, but aurochs weren't intimidated. They never ran. They stared down threats, and if that didn't work, they charged, lightning quick, head lowered in a tornado of hooves and horns, skewering and flinging in a signature move still used by Spanish bulls.

Somehow, people convinced this beast to tolerate us, live with us, and work for us, and through selective breeding, aurochs became the parent species for all domestic cattle. Eventually, aurochs, the original wild bull, went extinct, even as cattle spread everywhere.

More than the dog, cattle changed human life and the world. Using these "living tools" to haul, plow, and clothe and feed us, we successfully tamed wilderness itself and launched the agricultural revolution, transforming much of nature into a domesticated garden that would serve humans best.

Here's the irony today: Conservationists want the aurochs back because we need its help "rewilding" the very landscapes that domestic cattle helped us tame. And they are resurrecting the aurochs by trying to reverse domestication and undo all the hard work we went through to make a cooperative cow.

PLEISTOCENE REWILDING & KEYSTONE SPECIES

To save endangered species, heal environments, and lessen the effects of climate change, conservationists seek to rebuild and repair ecosystems. One thing that our current environmental crisis has shown is that we've tamed nature too well. Healthy habitats need more biodiversity and "wildness."

One approach is called Pleistocene rewilding. This refers to the last ice age that ended about 11,700 years ago. Of course, we can't literally rewind the clock and re-create what Earth was like back then. But the goal is to restore some of the lost biodiversity that existed before people started domesticating species, converting wilderness to fields and farms, and killing off so many of the giant species that once dominated ecosystems.

The aurochs was one of those giants. Like the woolly mammoth, aurochs were imposing beasts that helped shaped their environment—the temperate marshy forests and grasslands of Eurasia. And like the mammoth steppe after the mammoth disappeared, this biodiverse ecosystem suffered and changed once the aurochs was gone.

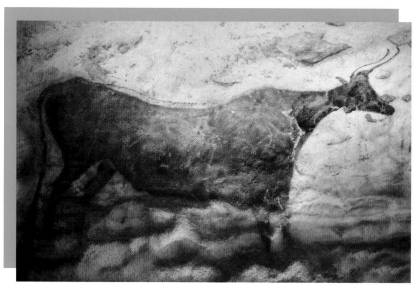

The aurochs is featured in many prehistoric cave paintings. This red aurochs, called "Cow with Collar," is from the Axial Gallery in France's famous Lascaux Cave. The estimated date it was painted is around 17,000 BCE.

Animals with that sort of impact are called keystone species. They play unique, irreplaceable roles that help hold the web of nature together. When they disappear, that web can unravel. In different ways, lions, rhinos, wolves, and elephants are all keystone species.

To rewild portions of Europe, conservationists are reintroducing large herds of grazing animals, such as water buffalo, wisent, musk oxen, and wild horses. This is the same approach as restoring the Siberian tundra, and as with the tundra, Europe needs its keystone species—the aurochs. Restoring ecosystems without replacing keystone species is like building a car without an engine: they won't run.

REVIVING A MENACE

Eventually, humans became the only threat aurochs couldn't overcome. People hunted the aurochs to extinction—not so much for food, though people did enjoy a good aurochs stew. Ever since ancient Greece, confronting and killing one of these irritable giants was considered an ultimate act of bravery.

Like the rhino, we became obsessed with shooting it. The last aurochs died—of natural causes—in 1627, becoming the first recorded extinction.

Yet the moment the aurochs was gone, people wanted it back. Eventually, people thought, If we can change wild animals into domestic ones through selective breeding, why can't we selectively breed domestic animals back into wild ones?

After all, the aurochs' genes live on in its domestic children.

One problem is that re-creating a wild species is about more than DNA. Domestication changes everything about the original animal. It changes behavior, making animals more docile and cooperative and less wary. Domestic animals are always smaller, they often retain juvenile characteristics into adulthood, they can be less fit and more prone to disease, and they can suffer from inbreeding due to a lack of genetic diversity. Domestic species are shaped by their dependence on us, and they can lose the vigor and behaviors that allow their wild parents to thrive in a world full of dangers.

For at least seventy years, those challenges haven't stopped people from using selective breeding to try to re-create the aurochs. The technique is called back-breeding, which involves crossing and recrossing (many, many times) various cattle breeds that exhibit specific aurochs-like traits, behaviors, and coloration. One day, the theory goes, the right combination of traits will emerge in the exact right ways and—*pop!*—an aurochs!

If scientists could clone an aurochs, they would, but this is impossible for the same reason that cloning a mammoth is impossible. No preserved living cells exist. Since we can't reproduce an exact genetic copy, a genuine aurochs is lost forever.

Nor can selective breeding literally go backward. Evolution only ever moves forward. Back-breeding has the *opposite* goal of domestication—it selectively breeds an animal to restore traits that humans got rid of, the ones that helped the animal live in the wild. However, the process can only create a new kind of wild cattle. That's why these cattle have been given a new name: *tauros*, which is the Greek word for "bull."

Thankfully, to rewild European landscapes, conservationists don't need an actual aurochs. They only need giant wild cattle that play the same ecosystem role. As Taurus Foundation director Ronald Goderie has promised, tauros "will look like an aurochs, live like an aurochs, behave, eat, mate, defecate, and eventually die like an aurochs."

Or as Henri Kerkdijk-Otten, the chair of the True Nature Foundation, says, "We want to create an aurochs for the twenty-first century."

IF YOU MEET TAUROS . . .

At least three different organizations are back-breeding aurochs-like wild cattle: the Dutch Tauros Programme (run by the Taurus

Since back-breeding is not cloning, tauros often look different from one another. These tauros from the Tauros Programme are among a growing variety of herds being released in multiple wildlife preserves across Europe.

Foundation), Auerrind in Germany, and the True Nature Foundation in the Netherlands. All continue to refine their breeding programs, but they are already placing their latest versions in select wilderness areas and nature preserves. Some are open to hikers and visitors.

Eventually, in another decade or so, the plan is for self-sustaining populations of tauros to roam free and become truly wild, without any interference or management by people. How well they replicate the aurochs' keystone role remains to be seen, but researchers are optimistic.

As with the woolly mammephant, what's far less certain is how people will coexist with them and how tauros will be regulated. One proposal is to treat some captive tauros like any other type of cattle and eat them as meat. Sales would provide income for conservation.

Heed this Yellowstone National Park sign if, by chance, you meet a tauros . . .

For most people, though, the more urgent question is what to do if someone meets tauros face-to-face in the wild. Even though researchers are trying to re-create the aurochs as closely as possible, they want to avoid restoring its legendary bad attitude. As Kerkdijk-Otten cautions, "We're talking about quite small wildlife parks, where people would be walking around among them with their kids. If children were tossed by cattle, the project would be finished."

At its own locations, the Tauros Programme provides a list of dos and don'ts for visitors should they encounter tauros. This commonsense advice applies to any wild animal encounter, such as bears or bison: keep your distance, back away if approached, don't come between a mother and child, and don't hike with a dog.

Then again, in 1602, someone with firsthand experience of aurochs wrote this:

> An aurochs is not afraid of humans and will not flee
> when a human being comes near. . . . If someone tries

to scare it by screaming or throwing something, this will not scare it in the least. . . . When it is standing in the road or somewhere else, one must go around it, even if one is driving a carriage, since it will not move off the road by itself. When challenged they become very hot-tempered, but if the person who has provoked it stretches out on the ground, nothing bad will happen to him, since they spare those who are stretched out, just like lions, with remarkable kindness.

Hmmm . . . one wonders if the author actually tried this, but if you find yourself facing an angry tauros, horns lowered in your direction, what have you got to lose?

CHAPTER 8

PASSENGER PIGEONS

n North America, four out of ten birds were once passenger pigeons, which was one of Earth's most prolific and successful birds. Their flocks reached inconceivable proportions. Millions and even billions could roll through the sky without pause for hours, even days, shadowing the sun and turning day into dusk.

Yet in the evolutionary blink of an eye—or about sixty years—people hunted them out of existence. This was hard to believe then, it remains astonishing now, and people still feel guilty.

The passenger pigeon isn't the only avian humans have knocked off either. We did in giant moa, great auks, heath hens, Carolina parakeets, the dodo—the poster bird of extinction—and many more.

What do you do after murdering a species? Until very recently, nothing. Extinction was the end. But using genetic engineering, researchers are attempting to resurrect the passenger pigeon, an effort

Passenger Pigeon
COLUMBA MIGRATORIA, Linn

Painter and naturalist John James Audubon created this famous depiction of a pair of passenger pigeons in 1829. In 1813, he witnessed an epic passenger pigeon flock in flight that blocked the sun as if it were an eclipse.

that embodies additional reasons people sometimes want to restore lost species: out of longing, regret, love, and an ethical urge to right human wrongs. Some people feel this way even knowing the new pigeon won't be exactly the same and might even be a royal pain to live with.

Ben Novak, the leader of the Great Passenger Pigeon Comeback, has said: "A new passenger pigeon may cause an internal debate in the on-looker, but when the piercing red iris meets the on-looker's gaze, in a moment of deep connection, it will remove all doubt, as if to say, 'I am the passenger pigeon reborn.' . . . Her story is far from over."

The passenger pigeon is returning—*the dead arise!*—but what kind of story will that be?

METEORS FROM HEAVEN

Those who witnessed the thunderous, undulating waves of passenger pigeons were left speechless and awestruck. Naturalist John James Audubon said a flock's "aerial evolutions . . . resembled the coils of a gigantic serpent," while up close, birds flew so fast that one "passes like a thought."

"Never have my astonishment, wonder, and admiration been so stirred," said Simon Pokagon, a Potawatomi chief, in the mid-1800s, "as when I have witnessed these birds drop from their course like meteors from heaven."

Like all meteors, they didn't land gently. Ecologist Aldo Leopold said they were "a biological storm," a "feathered tempest"—a tornado that ate everything and left devastation in its wake. A flock might blanket 100 square miles (260 sq. km) and pick clean every nut, fruit, grain, insect, and crop. They roosted so heavily in trees that limbs broke and entire trees gave out, while white dung fell thick as snow.

For millennia, Indigenous North Americans welcomed the birds' unexpected arrival—flocks migrated hundreds of miles and rarely landed in the same place twice—with celebratory hunts and long feasts. Passenger pigeons were a staple food and, apparently, good eating.

The last two living passenger pigeons, Martha (*shown*) and George, were named after George Washington, the first US president, and his wife. After Martha died, her body was preserved, and she remains a treasured specimen in the Smithsonian Institution.

From the 1600s on, European colonizers joined the fun, and they cooked pigeons in every possible way: stewed, fried, roasted, boiled, smoked, and baked in a pie.

All this might still be happening except that in the mid-1800s, pigeons became a moneymaking business, and amateur hunts to feed a family turned into professional slaughter for profit. Thousands of people arrived at a nesting, opened fire at once, and kept shooting till their stamina or ammunition ran out. Each time, millions of birds were killed, stuffed in barrels, and sent by train to market.

After a few decades, the passenger pigeon population collapsed. By 1907 the bird was extinct in the wild, and the last captive passenger pigeon, a female named Martha, died on September 1, 1914. People were stunned that such an iconic species was gone. Despite all the hunting, no one *wanted* to get rid of the passenger pigeon. That had seemed impossible.

THE CASE FOR RESURRECTION

Like Ben Novak, many people feel deep grief over this wanton, callous destruction, and they long to return this awe-inspiring bird to the skies.

This raises another ethical question: Is it ever okay to tinker with life just because the results would make us feel better? Some people say we have a moral obligation to help heal and restore species we've harmed, while others insist that emotions are never reason enough to justify creating (or changing) animals.

Yet in itself, caring is important. Emotions reflect our values and influence our choices. Caring inspires the dedication to meet challenges, solve complex problems, and make personal sacrifices. Some scientists say that re-creating certain extinct insects would be more ecologically beneficial than charismatic, beloved species like passenger pigeons or mammoths. Yet few spirits soar to imagine *insects reborn!* In bioengineering, as in all things, part of the challenge is recognizing our feelings, understanding our motivations, and adding them to our calculations.

The scientists and conservationists working to revive the passenger pigeon are certainly inspired by passion, but they also make an ecological case for resurrection: They believe that, like the aurochs and the woolly mammoth, the passenger pigeon was a keystone species whose presence shaped the landscape. A single bird could snuggle in your pocket, but en masse, passenger pigeons rivaled forest fires for the level of productive destruction they inflicted. According to Revive & Restore, this bird "quite possibly is the most important species for the future of conserving the woodland biodiversity of the eastern United States."

Passenger pigeons dispersed a forest's worth of seeds over hundreds of miles. This regeneration more than made up for the trees they destroyed. Plus, those destructive patches punched holes in forest canopies and led to restorative fires (which forests often need). As a result, a biodiverse mix of environments and species flourished. Further, all predators fed on the passenger pigeon— weasels, wolves, bears, owls, hawks—and all that pigeon poop enriched the soil.

In the past century, no bird has come along to play the passenger pigeon's ecosystem role, and eastern forests might be healthier with their old manager back.

Still, first things first: re-creating the passenger pigeon will take a miracle of biotechnology.

EVERY CHILD NEEDS A MOTHER

The method for making this bird uses CRISPR to cut and splice the DNA of a band-tailed pigeon—the passenger pigeon's closest living relative—with synthesized passenger pigeon DNA. After injecting this modified DNA into the germ cells (or reproductive cells) of rock pigeons, this will create rock pigeons with the sex organs of passenger pigeons. In science, this type of creature is called a chimera—or any bioengineered animal that contains genetically distinct cells from more than one species (just as the mythic Chimera was part lion, goat, and serpent).

These chimera birds will mate, and because their sperm and eggs are genetically from passenger pigeons, they will conceive a passenger pigeon chick (not a rock pigeon). Maybe that sounds impossible, but in 2019 the Great Passenger Pigeon Comeback proudly announced the creation of "the world's first successful pigeon germline chimera." They hope to hatch the first passenger pigeons by 2025. If this works, this process could potentially be used to de-extinct almost any bird.

Making a bird is only half the battle, though. Someone needs to teach this bird how to live like a passenger pigeon. If mammephants act like elephants, they'll probably replicate the woolly mammoth's ecosystem role, but no bird alive lives like the passenger pigeon. That's the whole point.

Ben Novak says, "It's their behavior, their propensity to live in dense flocks, that's the key in this experiment. If we can't get these pigeons to form flocks, we'll have failed."

So, even if scientists replicate the passenger pigeon's genome exactly and the new bird is a perfect physical replica—red iris and all—that isn't good enough. Genes are not behavior. If the bird doesn't act the same, it won't perform the role it's being remade for.

Novak is currently strategizing how to mother the new birds once they're born. It may be that raising a passenger pigeon is harder than making one.

REVIVING THE PAST TO REMAKE THE FUTURE

Let's say it works. Let's say it's 2030, and large flocks grace the skies, pummel the forests, and eat everything in sight.

Nineteenth-century farmers considered passenger pigeons "a perfect scourge." One Seneca Nation man said, "They came as a plague of locusts and devoured every sprouting plant." The acrid tang of excrement wafted for miles.

Imagine how people might react to this. People with new cars and backyard pools. People in airplanes. Will the government reimburse farmers who lose an entire crop or approve hunting so we can make pigeon pie? Will people be arrested who poison the bird as a pest?

If love inspires people to restore the passenger pigeon—a species that existed almost unchanged for twenty-two million years—how long will that love last? Even if passenger pigeons improve forest biodiversity, can we live with the mess?

All conservation efforts wrestle with questions of coexistence. They ask us to make sacrifices on behalf of nature: to make room for species and to accept living with some trouble. The real question is how much trouble. Even species we love can be a mixed blessing (see tigers and wolves). These questions only get more complicated when we are saving endangered species, rewilding landscapes, and de-extincting species.

For instance, since the passenger pigeon went extinct because of us, we need to figure out how to change human behavior (and write new laws) to avoid extinction again. Then we need to anticipate where and how this restored species will live. North America's eastern forests have changed a great deal over the last century. New passenger pigeons might love these forests, or they might decide, *Hey, look at all this farmland. Who needs a forest?*

Crossbreeding poses another danger. As with the coywolf, we can't stop wild animals from mating, so what if, say, city pigeons mated with this new-and-improved passenger pigeon and created a hybrid swarm or an even more troublesome breed of "superpigeon"? Would we eliminate all these hybrids . . . and how?

These aren't rhetorical questions. They need practical answers or at least attempted answers. We can never figure everything out ahead of time, and conservationists always hope, with every project, to create a healthy balance that allows ecosystems and all species to thrive. That could happen with the passenger pigeon. Yet conservation efforts rarely turn out exactly the way people expect. Even after anticipating all the possibilities, we'll still need to be flexible and adapt to what actually happens.

Bioengineering wild species is only the start of the story. De-extinction doesn't literally raise the dead, and rewilding doesn't re-create the past. All these efforts remake and shape our future. Every conservation decision reflects the species we value and the kind of world we want to live in.

Whether we tinker with species or not, we can't stop change. Whatever we do, evolution guarantees that nothing and no one will stay the same.

FROZEN ARKS: CRYOBANKING ON THE FUTURE

The extinction crisis is a battle we can't win. Human populations will keep growing and affecting nature, and the climate will keep changing. Species are built to adapt, but untold numbers won't evolve fast enough to survive. We don't know how many because we don't know how many species exist. Scientists have identified and named less than two million species, but they estimate the world holds more than fourteen million species, and maybe even one hundred million.

Here are the numbers so far: according to the International Union for Conservation of Nature (IUCN), the known modern extinctions for several major animal groups are birds, 159 species; mammals, 81; bony fishes, 62; amphibians, 35; and reptiles, 33. Maybe that doesn't sound too bad. But the IUCN calls these numbers a "significant underestimate," and the rate of extinctions is increasing. The numbers of threatened species—those at risk of going extinct—are also alarmingly high: birds, 1,486 species (14 percent of all birds); mammals, 1,244 (25 percent); bony fishes, 2,448 (8 percent); amphibians, 2,200 (41 percent); and reptiles, 1,409 (35 percent).

We don't have enough time, money, or conservationists to save all these animals. So people are doing the next best thing: saving their DNA.

In cryobanks—also known as "frozen arks"—scientists are preserving as much genetic information from as many species as possible before they disappear. They're called arks because this effort resembles the biblical story of Noah saving all the animals before the flood.

The concept is simple: preserve a sample of blood, hair, skin, egg, sperm, or bone in vats of liquid nitrogen at −321°F (−196°C) to halt all biological processes. DNA and living cells can remain viable this way for at least fifty years and maybe longer.

The rhino sperm used to fertilize eggs to help save the northern white rhino were cryopreserved in San Diego Zoo's Frozen Zoo—the largest cryobank in the world, with more than ten thousand specimens from a thousand species—over twenty years ago. The Frozen Ark at the University of Nottingham in England coordinates cryobanks around the globe. In twenty-two facilities, it estimates it has preserved forty-eight thousand samples from five thousand species. The Vertebrate Genomes Project has already sequenced ten thousand animal genomes, and it hopes to sequence up to sixty-six thousand.

Dr. Ann Clarke is a cofounder of the University of Nottingham's Frozen Ark project. Here, she checks a tray of cryo-preserved samples.

Those numbers give us hope. By preserving tissue samples, cells, genes, and genetic information, we are preserving the world's genetic biodiversity before it goes away. This can be used for any type of bioengineering project: to save endangered species, to increase genetic diversity, to resurrect extinct species, to modify animals against disease, to improve livestock, to clone animals, to make medicine, to devise new materials, and to aid human health—plus all the other uses we have yet to dream up.

Extinction really isn't the end of the story anymore.

OLD McDONALD HAD A CLONE

Nothing creeps out some people more than the idea of genetically modified (GM) food, or what has been disparagingly called Frankenfood. But every domestic plant and animal—corn, wheat, apples, chickens, cows—has already been genetically altered through domestication and selective breeding to be bigger, tastier, and easier to raise and grow.

As molecular biologist Nina Fedoroff writes, "Our civilization rests, in fact, on a history of tinkering with nature, on making the earth say beans, as Thoreau so eloquently said, instead of grass."

Part 3 explores how the new tools of genetic engineering are allowing us to tinker with livestock and domestic animals, and how these efforts might help us solve a trio of related problems: how to feed a growing world population (over 7.7 billion and counting) while fostering a healthier environment and better animal welfare. Genetic engineering in agriculture could help feed the world and save the planet . . . but people still wonder, Should genetically engineered animals be dinner?

Collectively, this might be one of the most important decisions we make.

CHAPTER 9

DOLLY & THE CLONES

Cloning in agriculture is becoming standard practice. Cloned livestock might be calmly chewing grass in your town, and you wouldn't know by looking. Really, there's nothing strange about cloned livestock . . . except the way they're made.

DOWN ON THE CLONE FARM

Entire farms could be populated with all the domestic animals we've already cloned: cows, sheep, pigs, goats, horses, mules, rabbits, dogs, and cats. And we've also cloned deer, camels, buffalo, frogs, ferrets, mice, rats, and more. About the only traditional farm animals people haven't cloned so far are chickens and other poultry, since birds are more difficult to clone.

The first clone made from an adult animal was Dolly, a sheep, in 1996, and thousands of cloned farm animals have followed.

Most often, ranchers clone their best animals—the biggest, healthiest, and most fertile individuals, the ones that resist disease and

Here are two of the first five pigs ever cloned from adult cells. They were born in March 2000 and created by PPL Therapeutics, a spin-off company of Scotland's Roslin Institute, which created Dolly the sheep.

produce the most milk or the best meat—but not to eat those animals. Clones are expensive (a cloned cow costs about $20,000), and farmers are running a business. Every investment must help them turn a profit.

Unless clones are intended as working or show animals, cloned livestock are usually used for breeding. The clones mate in the normal way, and their superior genes create high-quality offspring. Then those offspring are used for food. Since the age of domestication, farmers have been amateur geneticists who selectively breed their prized animals to improve a herd's genetics. Cloning ensures that great genes get passed on exactly.

To improve livestock production, ranchers usually treat cloning like any other assisted reproductive technology, which refers to any and all reproductive techniques. Cloning doesn't freak them out. Several cloned cows and steers have won state-fair competitions. Whether farmers decide to clone usually depends on a cost-benefit analysis, not philosophical questions about the nature of the animal.

Occasionally, cloned livestock are used for food, such as when a cloned cow or bull becomes too old to breed. Ordering a burger or ham sandwich? That meat could be from a clone. In 2008 the FDA declared that food from cloned cattle, pigs, and goats "is as safe to eat as food from any other cattle, swine, or goat," and it doesn't need labeling as genetically modified or "made from clones."

As farmers like to say, a clone is "an identical twin born later." It's a genetic copy of the original animal. Cloning is certainly genetic engineering, but a cloned cow is 100 percent cow.

COUNTING SHEEP: WHAT IS A CLONE?

That said, a clone isn't *actually* a 100 percent identical twin. It's not a *perfect* copy. Genetics are more complicated than a copy machine.

To understand what a clone is, let's consider Dolly. In 1996 scientists took a single cell from an adult ewe and used its DNA to make a new embryo. They took a specialized somatic cell from the sheep's udder (but they could have taken a cell from anywhere). The most common type of cell, somatic cells are body cells that are programmed to do only one job: to become bone, organs, muscle, hair, skin, blood, and so on.

Scientists removed this cell's nucleus, which contained its DNA, and implanted it into the unfertilized egg cell of another sheep. The egg cell—which had had its own nucleus removed—was an unspecialized stem cell. Unlike somatic cells, stem cells are reproductive cells that have the ability to turn into any type of cell. Then, as embryos develop, stem cells differentiate into specialized somatic or body cells according to their genetic instructions, creating a person, rabbit, or cow—or whatever their DNA tells them to be.

With Dolly, once the somatic-cell nucleus was inserted, the egg cell—amazingly—transformed the nucleus back into a stem cell. Then the cell was literally shocked with electricity to start dividing—just like in *Frankenstein*—and the viable egg was implanted into the womb of a surrogate ewe. Then nature took over: the embryo grew into a fetus and was eventually born as Dolly, the world's first clone from an adult animal.

This is called somatic cell nuclear transfer. The reason it doesn't produce an exact copy is because it mixes material from two different cells: the DNA in the nucleus of the animal being cloned and the mitochondrial DNA in the "jelly" of the egg cell from the other animal. Mitochondrial DNA is a separate genome, distinct from the

The sheep that Dolly was cloned from had died before Dolly was born. Since the cells used for cloning were taken from the original ewe's preserved mammary glands, cheeky researchers named the clone after the famed country singer Dolly Parton.

DNA in a cell's nucleus. So the female who donates the egg cell adds her mitochondrial DNA to the clone.

In contrast, the reason identical twins are "identical" is because the same fertilized egg divides into two embryos. So both embryos have completely identical DNA.

But DNA isn't everything. How genes express themselves—epigenetics—also makes a difference. In the womb, a fetus can be influenced by the environment and the mother's diet. Even after the baby is born, early experiences can affect when certain genes turn on and off or interact.

In effect, a clone has *three* parents: the animal whose cell nucleus provides the DNA, the animal that donates the egg and mitochondrial DNA, and the female that carries the embryo to term and gives birth.

Clones often look like mirror images of the animal that provides the nuclear DNA, even exhibiting identical gestures and behaviors. Sometimes, though, clones *are* slightly different. And when somatic cell nuclear transfer is used between two different species—such as when cloning one rhino species by using an egg and surrogate mother from another rhino species—what's born will be an even less exact clone.

THE COSTS OF CLONING

The breeding of livestock is often (but not always) managed. Farmers regularly use assisted reproductive technologies, such as artificial insemination, embryo transfer, and in vitro fertilization (in which eggs are fertilized outside the body and transferred to a surrogate female).

But, while cloning might be just another assisted reproductive technology, cloning is different and more expensive in terms of animal welfare.

To make Dolly, scientists modified 277 eggs, resulting in twenty-nine viable embryos. These were implanted into thirteen surrogate mothers, but only one embryo successfully matured into a cloned sheep: Dolly. Cloning the first horse required *841* embryos.

Despite improvements, this level of failure remains common. Lots of things can go wrong during this process. Embryos might not develop properly or implant correctly in the womb, resulting in miscarriages and still births. Complications and congenital diseases—like abnormal organ development—can cause animals to die hours, days, or weeks after being born. Cattle and sheep can sometimes develop large offspring syndrome, in which the fetus grows too large in the womb, causing pain for the mother.

All reproductive technologies have these issues, but they occur far more often with cloning. This is why animal welfare groups often protest cloned livestock: the price in animal suffering can be high.

Once clones become adults, they tend to be "perfectly healthy" (according to the FDA), and their offspring show no problems.

Ranchers debate the merits and ethics of cloning. It's not always worth the cost, but some feel it can be, depending on the animal, how they're used, and the circumstances. These are questions we all should ask: Is cloning livestock always OK, never OK, or only for certain reasons? Then, so long as an animal is healthy and safe to eat, does it matter if our food comes from clones?

Herself a proud mother, Dolly gave birth to six lambs, including Bonnie (*shown*). After living over six years, Dolly was euthanized in 2003 after developing lung cancer (unrelated to cloning).

CHAPTER 10

SUPER PIGS & HORNLESS CATTLE

Have you heard the urban legend about KFC?

For decades, internet stories have claimed the fast-food chain was brewing featherless, beakless chickens with extra legs and wings to get more meat from each bird and lower costs.

Don't believe it. This fake news uses doctored photos and plays on our worst fears: that genetic tinkering is making monsters for profit.

Yet the fake photos show real featherless chickens. Featherlessness can be a naturally occurring mutation, and Israeli researchers once crossbred a featherless bird with stewing chickens to make a more heat-tolerant "naked chicken" that might be easier to raise in hot countries. These birds were studied but never adopted by the industry.

The unsettling, even alarming truth is that we really *can* modify animals in almost any way we choose, but to effectively evaluate whether genetic engineering provides a positive solution that helps

In 2002, when researchers at Hebrew University in Jerusalem created "naked chickens," they claimed the birds might be more heat-tolerant, environmentally friendly, and lower in calories. Public shock and concern over the welfare of the chickens ended the experiment.

solve the urgent problems of agriculture, we must be wary of alarmism, exaggerations, and falsehoods.

SUPER PIG: SAVING THE ENVIRONMENT

Worldwide, humans raise a lot of pigs. We eat about a billion every year, or about twenty-three million every week.

Those pigs produce a lot of waste. Pig manure can cause serious environmental damage. It contains high amounts of nitrogen and phosphorus, which can pollute lakes and rivers, cause algae blooms, and harm ecosystems.

So, in 1999 researchers created the Enviropig. This transgenic pig—containing genetic material from mice and *E. coli* bacteria—can better digest the phosphorus in its food. This lessens the amount of phosphorus in its poop.

A less-polluting pig—that sounds good, right? Yet no one wanted it. Farmers feared no one would eat a bioengineered animal—and environmental groups protested that an "environmentally friendly pig" would only encourage farmers to crowd swine and pollute even more.

Eventually, the project was dropped. Cecil Forsberg, the Enviropig's coinventor, said, "I had the feeling in seven or eight or nine years that transgenic animals probably would be acceptable. But I was wrong."

In 2018 Chinese researchers tried again and actually improved on the Enviropig: The latest version also digests nitrogen and grows faster. Studies show that compared to regular pigs, this "super pig" excretes almost half the amount of nitrogen and phosphorus in its manure, and its growth rate is almost 25 percent faster.

This pig creates less pollution and eats less, reducing its environmental impact. And these pigs seem healthy, showing no behavioral or reproductive issues.

However, just like in the United States, people in China are reluctant to eat transgenic animals, so it's unclear if this pig will ever be approved for consumption and grown by industry.

Another major environmental problem genetic engineering might help solve is belching cattle. Cow burps release methane, a main greenhouse gas. Reducing this methane would help minimize climate change. But if people won't eat genetically modified cattle, engineering a "methane-free cow" wouldn't make a difference.

DISEASE-FREE LIVESTOCK: IMPROVING ANIMAL HEALTH

We can also genetically engineer domestic animals to resist certain diseases. This also helps protect people from the illnesses we get from livestock.

The devastating nature of livestock diseases is partly related to domestication and selective breeding, which lessens genetic diversity and can make livestock less fit than their wild cousins. Of course, selective breeding—especially guided by genome sequencing—is also used to boost genetic diversity and improve livestock health. But genetic engineering is more direct and effective: it can target specific diseases, engineer resistance, and might eliminate some diseases entirely.

One research group's proposal is to isolate the warthog genes that resist African swine fever and insert them into domestic pigs. In Europe and China, this virus is particularly devastating and can destroy entire domestic pig populations.

Another proposal is to alter the genes of chickens to make them immune to influenza, or so that if they get the flu, they can't spread the disease. When bird flus infect a few individuals, farmers can be forced to kill millions of birds to stop the infection from spreading. Bird and mammal coronaviruses can also make people sick. These viruses are a primary source of the common cold, but they can also become extremely deadly, such as the SARS outbreak in 2003 and, even more dramatically, the worldwide COVID-19 pandemic that began in 2020.

The viruses typically first arise in wild animals, and then migrate to livestock and humans, so engineering resistance to viruses in livestock won't end the spread of viruses among people, but it could minimize it.

With pigs, another major problem is porcine reproductive and respiratory syndrome, a virus that occurs during pregnancy and causes pneumonia in piglets. It has no cure, spreads quickly, and costs the US pork industry about half a billion dollars every year. Yet by removing a particular protein in pigs—by modifying a few bits of DNA—mothers show resistance to this virus and give birth to healthy piglets.

A health issue with dairy cows is mastitis, an infection of the udders. Mastitis can affect any female mammal—including humans—but this can be a major problem in agriculture. Dairy cows with mastitis must be removed from production, costing the dairy industry about $1.7 billion a year.

In 2000 scientists created the first genetically engineered cow to resist mastitis, but the effort was abandoned because the costs to meet federal regulations were too high, and everyone worried that customers would never drink the cows' milk.

HORNLESS CATTLE: IMPROVING ANIMAL WELFARE

Another ethical concern in agriculture is animal welfare. So long as people raise animals for food products and meat, the goal should be to treat those animals as humanely as possible while they are alive and in our care. This includes preventing "needless suffering," or pain and distress that could be minimized or avoided by changing farming practices. Modern agriculture is sometimes disparaged as "factory farming" because it can prioritize convenience and industrial efficiency over the welfare of animals.

People originally learned how to modify wild animals for our benefit through domestication. Genetic engineering offers the possibility of modifying domestic animals for *their own* benefit even

Dairy cows that have been genetically altered to be hornless (*center and right*) look no different than their horned counterparts, aside from missing horns, and the genetic changes don't affect their milk.

though we are still using them for ours. Researchers are experimenting with how to alter livestock to eliminate certain painful practices that would improve animal lives. Two examples are dehorning dairy cows and castrating young male pigs.

The horns on Holstein cows are long and dangerous to other cows and to people. Aurochs, their wild parent, developed epic horns to fight lions and dire wolves, but dairy cows don't need defensive weapons. Their lives wouldn't change without them. So dairy farmers often prevent horns from growing by burning them with irons or chemicals. This hurts the animal.

Since some cattle exhibit hornless mutations, these cattle could be selectively bred with dairy cows until hornlessness became dominant among most dairy cows. Yet this approach would take a long time and be inexact and incomplete. Using genetic "scissors," scientists have already engineered a dairy cow that will never grow horns. But because of continued public resistance to GM foods, dairy farmers have refused to adopt these permanently hornless cattle.

Farmers also routinely castrate male piglets. This reduces male aggression as adults, and it eliminates "boar taint," or an unpleasant odor and taste related to male hormones. By disabling certain pig genes, researchers can prevent puberty from happening. This would eliminate the need for castration—which is painful for the pig and unpleasant for the farmer.

ETHICS ISN'T ABOUT TOOLS BUT HOW WE USE THEM

Genetic engineering might solve certain agricultural problems we can't solve otherwise. In many ways, it might make feeding ourselves healthier, more sustainable, less polluting, and even kinder to animals. These tools can also be used in ways that benefit business: to maximize productivity, ease labor, lower expenses, and increase profits.

Ultimately, the tools we use are less important than how we use them. That *how* includes asking what purpose genetic engineering serves and who benefits. Sometimes, the answer could be everyone. Creating a disease-resistant Enviropig that never needs castrating helps the pig, the environment, human health, and the farmer's business.

Solving the enormous crises facing agriculture—how to feed our growing population using less land and creating less pollution—will require all kinds of solutions. Biotechnology isn't a magic wand, and on its own, changing farm animals will never be enough. To overcome the biggest challenges, human society and the agricultural industry also need to change.

The 2017 movie *Okja* raises this dilemma. It's about a gigantic, genetically enhanced "super pig" that will "leave a minimal footprint on the environment, consume less feed, and produce less excretions." While the movie's super pig is a cuddly, unrealistic giant, it sounds like the Enviropig. They have the same purpose.

But in the movie, the evil agricultural corporation does exactly what critics fear: They cram the pigs into tight pens, increase animal suffering, and do even more harm—all to make a buck. In this story, selfish, greedy human motives undermine what might, in theory, be a genuinely better animal for the world.

Like good science fiction, *Okja* is a cautionary tale that imagines what could go wrong, but the movie is not necessarily our fate. We can choose what to do and why. We can decide when it's safe, practical, effective, and ethical to genetically engineer farm animals, and when we must also (or instead) regulate business, change agricultural practices, and even change our attitudes. If we want to foster a more sustainable world, we will need to use every tool we have.

CHAPTER 11
FRANKENFISH

The first transgenic animal to be approved for human consumption is the AquAdvantage salmon. This Atlantic salmon is mixed with genetic material from a Chinook salmon and another fish, the ocean pout.

First developed by AquaBounty in the early 1990s, the fish underwent decades of painstaking review by the FDA, which declared it safe to eat in 2015. Nevertheless, further regulatory hurdles and public resistance kept the fish from being sold in the United States until June 2021, when the first transgenic salmon were grilled and served in US restaurants, and one (but only one) US seafood distributor agreed to sell it.

TRANSGENESIS: LIFE, REMIXED

Transgenesis refers to adding new genes or DNA sequences into an animal's genome. The new sequences could be either modified DNA from the same species or foreign genetic material from a different species. The AquAdvantage salmon mixes genes from different types of fish, but experiments have included inserting a fish gene into a tomato and moth genes into an apple.

The thought of this is enough to make some people lose their appetite, but individual genes don't embody the whole plant or animal. Specific genes perform specific functions, and like parts in a car, they can be swapped, retooled, and tinkered with. As molecular biologist Nina Fedoroff writes, "It is as impossible to attach the quality of being an insect to a protein as it is to attach the quality of being a car to a spark plug. There is no way a gene from a fish could make a tomato 'fishy.'"

Nor do moth genes make apples "mothy." Researchers wanted to see if a little moth DNA might protect apples from fire blight (a bacterial disease), and they wanted to see if a flounder's "antifreeze gene" might protect a tomato from frost. But neither of these experiments were ever brought to market. This is the same process as adding warthog genes to domestic pigs to protect them from African swine fever. Transgenesis doesn't create a hybrid, a new being that combines the entire genomes of two species, like a coywolf or liger. Adding foreign genes gives an animal or plant a specific new trait that's related to those genes, nothing else. It's the same car. It just drives a little differently.

The AquAdvantage salmon was created by taking part of the ocean pout's antifreeze gene—its "promoter"—and using that to replace the "promoter" in the Chinook salmon's growth-hormone gene, and then inserting this novel, foreign DNA into an Atlantic salmon. This genetic tinkering supercharges the Atlantic salmon's growth by allowing the AquAdvantage salmon to grow year-round—even in cold weather, which wild salmon don't do. On average,

The transgenic AquAdvantage salmon looks like a normal salmon, but it grows much faster using fewer resources, which minimizes the environmental impact of farm-raised fish.

AquAdvantage salmon eat 25 percent less food, and yet they reach market weight, about 10 pounds (4.5 kg), in eighteen months. That's almost twice as fast as conventionally farmed salmon.

IS IT A FRANKENFISH OR A SUPER FISH?

Skeptics and critics have dubbed this transgenic animal a Frankenfish, while others consider it a potential ecological superhero. Like a transgenic super pig, this animal might feed more people using fewer resources and with less impact on the environment.

In efficiency, or the amount of resources needed to raise animals for food, this salmon is twice as efficient as chickens, three times better than pigs, and eight times better than cows. Farmed salmon also reduce the impact on wild salmon, which are being overfished. Many wild salmon populations are endangered, and climate change and habitat loss are making this worse.

AquaBounty's system is also eco-friendlier than traditional salmon farms, which raise fish in sea cages and fly the fish, mainly from Norway and Chile, to US markets. AquaBounty's fish are produced on land at two facilities, in Indiana and Canada. This reduces the carbon emissions from transportation. They also recycle virtually all the water they use, minimizing waste. One report estimated that the overall carbon footprint of this approach might be less than half of conventional fish farms.

As AquaBounty's CEO Sylvia Wulf said, "Our fish was really designed for land-based farming."

REGULATION: ASKING HARD QUESTIONS

This fish was basically ready to eat almost thirty years ago, but public resistance to genetically modified foods, political and scientific caution, and regulatory confusion have kept it out of grocery stores. Just as hybrid wild animals don't fit our species categories and conservation laws, bioengineered animals don't fit the regulatory categories of the food industry. Federal agencies have wrestled with how to define GM food animals and how to appropriately test them for safety.

Years ago, as the FDA struggled with this, it decided to classify any genetic alteration in animals the same as a "veterinary drug." Since drugs are considered anything that changes an animal, and genetic engineering definitely changes the animal, this seemed logical. This category also requires extremely strict oversight, which helps ensure these experiments are safe. But meeting these regulations is so time-consuming and expensive that it has, in effect, strangled development. Only large companies can afford to try.

"Regulation is important," says animal geneticist Alison Van Eenennaam, who helped develop hornless cattle. "Looking at these things carefully is necessary. But not at the exclusion of all innovation, ever." Further, "this idea that DNA variation is a drug is absolutely nonsensical."

Most scientists agree that drugs and gene editing are inherently different and need to be regulated differently. They say regulations should focus on the safety of the genetic change (not on what method or technology was used), and GM animals should be regulated more like GM plants (which are reviewed differently).

Those issues aside, to approve the AquAdvantage salmon, the FDA needed to answer two essential questions: First, is the fish healthy and safe to eat, and second, could it harm other fish or the environment if it escaped? These types of questions need to be asked about every genetically altered creation.

For the first question, the FDA found "no biologically relevant differences" between this fish and other salmon, nor do the genetic changes harm the fish. Simply put, different though they may be, these are healthy salmon. For the second question, AquaBounty genetically modifies their fish in other ways to ensure that only sterile female fish are hatched. Their two facilities are also landlocked, and the fish are

AquaBounty raises their salmon in tanks inside warehouses to prevent fish from escaping into local waters. In the future, if more transgenic fish are approved for consumption, this type of land-based aquaculture may become more common.

raised entirely in tanks. So, the FDA decided there is an "extremely low likelihood" that fish could escape into waters or survive if they did, let alone reproduce with wild salmon.

Waiting for the FDA to reach these conclusions nearly bankrupted AquaBounty. And without the current regulatory process, it's possible that all the altered livestock in chapter 10 might already be oinking, mooing, and clucking on farms.

Geneticists like Van Eenennaam feel that these regulations need to be changed and that they exemplify how we as a society are too afraid of biotechnology that could radically improve our world.

Figuring out how much regulation is needed, and what type, is the tricky part. Genetic engineering is still so new that people have a hard time deciding what reasonable caution looks like. For instance, in 2019 the FDA discovered some "unintended" bacterial DNA in the first genetically altered hornless cattle, which were created in 2015 as test cases. This caused a minor uproar, but further research showed this DNA doesn't harm the animals, and newer methods probably make this overlooked gene-editing error easy to avoid. In theory, then, this was an example of how effective regulation works: it helps us discover mistakes, determine whether modified animals are safe, and ideally approve them when they are.

THE FINAL JUDGE: YOU

AquaBounty says its salmon are delicious, but you don't have to take their word for it.

If you get a chance, try some and decide for yourself. Customers always have the last word, and if people don't buy or eat genetically modified foods, companies won't make them.

And lots of people say they won't eat this fish—or any GM foods.

The anti-GM movement has been fighting to stop the approval, use, and consumption of most (if not all) genetically modified plants and animals for decades. In 2013 one poll found that 75 percent of Americans said they'd never eat bioengineered fish, and ongoing protests against the AquAdvantage salmon have led many US grocery chains to pledge not to stock it. For environmentalists, one particular issue is that they don't trust that these salmon are 100 percent sterile and can't escape. If they did escape, this might endanger wild salmon populations, which some Native American communities depend on.

Not everyone feels this way. In Canada, AquaBounty's transgenic salmon have been sold in stores since 2017 without any labels (which Canada doesn't require). And so far . . . no catastrophes, no mass protests. One marine biologist who reviewed the fish for the FDA said, "In twenty or twenty-five years, we're all going to be eating genetically modified animal products."

Whether they know it or not, most people are eating genetically modified plants already. In the mid-1990s, about the same time that the AquAdvantage salmon was developed, the first GM foods were approved for consumption. These included "Bt corn," which was bioengineered with a bacteria gene that acts like a natural insecticide. By 2020 in America, more than half of all corn and 90 percent of soybeans were genetically modified.

And slowly, more transgenic animals will be approved for use and consumption. In 2020 the FDA approved the second: the GalSafe pig. This animal was modified to avoid causing an allergic reaction some people have to red meat.

Fear of new technology is common. At first, people feared telephones, television, and computers—now all three fit in a back pocket. So when will anxiety over bioengineering give way to ho-hum, what's-for-dinner acceptance? Maybe not tomorrow or next year, but one day, it's not hard to imagine that the main thing people will care about is whether an animal is healthy and safe to eat. What won't matter is where that animal's genes come from.

As Fedoroff writes, "The challenge of the coming decades is to limit the destructive effects of agriculture even as we continue to coax ever more food from the earth. It is a task made less daunting by new knowledge and new methods—if we use them wisely."

SYNTHETIC BIOLOGY: DIY REVOLUTION OR DISASTER?

To many, the ultimate example of playing god with bioengineering is synthetic biology. This refers to a range of techniques for creating and recombining DNA to make organisms that don't and could never exist in nature. Essentially, it's building life from scratch by arranging genes like Lego blocks—or even writing new strands of DNA letter by letter—to make unique, once-impossible creations.

Synthetic biology doesn't make new animals (not yet!), since bodies are agonizingly complex. Synthetic biology currently works mostly with bacteria and microorganisms, but we can do a lot with a one-celled organism.

Modified bacteria can turn algae and sewage into biofuel. Synthetic microbes can produce plastics, chemicals, flavors, new materials, and beneficial drugs. Engineered bacteria can produce spider silk proteins—making spider goats unnecessary (see chapter 15). Synthetic biologists are also figuring out how to grow meat separate from animals.

The potential exists for synthetic biology to solve all kinds of problems in medicine, manufacturing, the environment, agriculture, and more.

Best of all, anyone can do it.

DIY biohacking has become a global movement—one driven by citizen scientists and biotech rebels who want to make the tools, genomes, and know-how of bioengineering available to everyone. Local DIY bio labs operate by the same open-source attitude that inspired early computer programming. If the first Apple computer could be born in a garage, why not the next biotech revolution?

Biological organisms can be programmed like software, and using computers, anyone can read, store, alter, and write genetic sequences easily and cheaply. One popular method uses BioBricks. These interlocking genetic components—or standardized biological parts—can be fit together in any combination. Then a mail-order biotech lab can prepare your design.

If you're a teen who wants to make genes, check out iGEM—the International Genetically Engineered Machine Competition. Held annually at MIT, iGEM gives university and high school students "the opportunity to push the boundaries of synthetic biology."

Are there dangers? Of course! Just like computer hackers can develop computer viruses, nefarious biohackers could create a biological virus. Someone could download the genetic blueprint for, say, malaria, tweak it, and release it. This is one reason people argue for limits on the type of genome information that's shared online. Synthetic biology has the potential to both cure and create disease.

Another fear is the "green goo" nightmare: What if a dangerous substance escapes someone's garage lab by accident? When anyone can practice synthetic biology at home, people worry about bioerror as much as bioterror. Synthetic biology could revolutionize our world, but no one wants life to imitate Kurt Vonnegut's novel *Cat's Cradle*, in which the fictional compound ice-nine—*whoops!*—slips free and freezes everything.

PART 4

WHAT KIND OF PET SHOULD I MAKE?

What would Theodor Geisel, the famed Dr. Seuss,
Think of the animals we are now setting loose
To be pets in our yards, companions in our homes,
Some of them glowing, some of them cloned,
Some shrunk so small they fit in your pocket,
Some double-muscled and faster than rockets?
What would he think—what do *you*—
Of all the mixed-up creatures in our bioengineered zoo?
Are they even too strange for Gerald McGrew?
Dr. Seuss made up Yinks, Whos, Wockets, and Zax,
Sneetches, a Grinch, and an angry Lorax,
But he never imagined what we're making today.
If he did, would he think *yay* or *nay*? Either way,
He'd probably say take care of them, don't fear,
For a creature's a creature, no matter how weird.

CHAPTER 12

MR. GREEN GENES

The question sounds like the setup to a bad joke:

Why are we making glowing bunnies?

Because rabbits can't hold flashlights.

In fact, scientists first made a glowing animal for the same reason people made the first ligers: curiosity. To discover what was possible.

Now we can make any animal glow, even humans if we want, and the list of glowing creatures we've created includes fish, cats, dogs, pigs, sheep, mice, monkeys . . .

Which raises another question: Who wants a glowing animal . . . and why?

SCIENTISTS: USING NATURE'S HIGHLIGHTER

Lots of organisms emit light. At dusk, fireflies pulse a beacon of love to attract a mate. In the pitch-black deep sea, anglerfish dangle a bioluminescent barbel to mesmerize prey. Beetles, bacteria, fungi, corals, worms, jellyfish, and thousands of other species glow.

In the 1980s, as scientists first experimented with gene editing in animals, they struggled with an obvious problem: genes are hard to see. Proteins are too small even for electron microscopes. Tinkering with genes is almost like working in the dark. It's hard to tell if you are successful unless the animal that's grown from the changed cell exhibits the new trait in a way that can be seen or measured.

So scientists wondered, What if they could isolate the light-producing protein certain species make naturally and add that to a cell? If it worked, the animal that grew from that cell would be a different color, and they would know they'd succeeded.

The first glowing monkey, pig, dog, and cat (named Mr. Green Genes) were test cases. They were the first transgenic animals of their kind, and they were created to see if it was possible to insert foreign genes from another species into an animal.

Making an animal glow might seem silly, but it proved to our eyes that transgenesis worked.

Scientists soon discovered that they could attach this glowing protein to virtually any other added gene or gene edit they were making. This was like highlighting the genetic change without affecting that change or harming the animal. If the altered animal glows, this visually confirms that genetic editing was successful. This highlighting technique—attaching a glowing protein to added or changed genes—has sparked a revolution in scientific research in fields as diverse as medicine, molecular biology, agriculture, and environmental studies.

The most commonly used green fluorescent protein (GFP) is from the *Aequorea victoria* jellyfish, and scientists have since modified it (and used other glowing proteins) to make even more colors, like yellow, red, blue, and gold.

These cats are from a university in South Korea. The cat on the left has been modified to possess a red fluorescent protein. The other cat (*right*) was cloned but does not possess any GFP modifications.

Are glowing animals OK? They seem healthy and normal—aside from glowing. And GFP only *glows* under ultraviolet light. In regular light, the modified animals look like any garden-variety dog, cat, or bunny—but with an off-color tinge to the skin.

Using special equipment, scientists can even "see" GFP-tagged genes inside an animal's body. This is why GFP is used in virtually every type of medical research. For example, scientists can study the progression of diseases—such as the internal spread of cancerous tumors—without needing to perform surgery or kill the animal. They instead track the growth of the GFP-tagged cells. Avoiding surgery both improves research and is more humane.

"GFP is used in thousands of experiments every day," writes chemistry professor Marc Zimmer. "GFP is becoming a commonplace scientific tool—just like a microscope . . . or even a test tube."

For researchers, glowing bunnies are just . . . *yawn* . . . part of a day's work.

ARTISTS: CREATING SHOCK AND EWWWW

Of course, most people aren't scientists. The first time someone sees a yellow beagle, a red pig, or a green monkey, it's often shocking. It seems . . . wrong. But is it?

That's the question that artist Eduardo Kac wanted people to ask when, in 2000, he exhibited a photograph of a glowing bunny he named Alba. Kac got Alba from a French lab that had made at least 150 glowing rabbits. "I will never forget the moment when I first held her in my arms," wrote Kac. "Alba . . . was lovable and affectionate and an absolute delight. . . . She immediately awoke in me a strong and urgent sense of responsibility for her well-being."

In the photograph, Kac enhanced the "glow" so that not only Alba's eyes, paws, and whiskers were neon green, but her fur seemed radioactive, even though hair doesn't glow on GFP animals.

Scientist Tomoko Nakanishi admires three, two-day-old glowing mice at Osaka University in 1997.

When people saw this photo, they flipped out. The artwork inspired shock, disgust, and awe. People wanted to know if the bunny was real, how it was possible, who was doing it—and *why*?

This public uproar was exactly what Kac wanted. By shocking people, he hoped to raise awareness about bioengineering and to spark discussions about what is right and wrong, OK and not OK—much like the purpose of this book.

Kac said society needs "a serious debate that acknowledges both the problems and benefits of the technology," since "a complete ban on all forms of genetic research would prevent the development of much-needed cures for the many devastating diseases that now ravage human and nonhumankind." Equally important for Kac, though, was that Alba was healthy and loved. He wanted to keep her indefinitely as a pet (though this didn't happen).

Others felt the same way. In the "Alba Guestbook (2000)," one person wrote: "How can I get this kind of rabbit at home?"

PEOPLE: LOVING OUR MONSTERS

You can't get a glowing bunny as a pet. At least not yet. But you *can* buy transgenic glowing zebra fish, or GloFish, as they're called.

Like all other GFP animals, glowing zebra fish were first created by scientists for a serious purpose—to signal polluted waters by glowing in the presence of toxins. Once a glowing fish existed, though, some people thought: *That's cool! I want one!* And if people want and are willing to pay for something, then some company will try to produce it and sell it. That's exactly what happened.

In 2003 GloFish became the first transgenic animal approved for sale in the United States. The FDA could find no reason to reject them: the fish are healthy, they aren't used as food, and even if they escape into waterways, they don't pose a genuine danger to wild species. They *might* mate and pass their glowing genes to other fish, but the glow only appears under ultraviolet light. Even if it were visible to other fish, it would probably flash like an Eat Me sign to predators, thus ending the problem.

Just as important, there have been no public protests over transgenic glowing pet fish. People seem to accept and enjoy them. Maybe that's because many fish and sea creatures already come rainbow-hued, and even glow, so bright colors seem natural.

Well, guess what? Some mammals also glow naturally. We just didn't realize it until recently. One night in 2018, a flying squirrel flew past a researcher's fluorescent light in a streak of glowing fuchsia. This discovery sent scientists scurrying with black lights looking for

Since 2003, GloFish has sold a variety of small glowing transgenic fish for home aquariums. Colors include "cosmic blue," "electric green," "galactic purple," "moonrise pink," and "sunburst orange."

more species, and they keep finding them. So far, the list of glowing mammals includes flying squirrels (pink), platypuses (sea green), springhares (red orange), opossums (many colors), wombats (blue), Tasmanian devils (blue), flying foxes (blue), and the quills of hedgehogs and echidnas (bright white).

Researchers have no idea why these animals glow, what purpose this serves, or if the animals can even see it. Yet apparently, glowing mammals aren't so strange after all. Researchers have yet to find any rabbits, dogs, or cats that glow naturally, but if, under certain light, flying squirrels are bubblegum pink, is it wrong to want your own Mr. Green Genes?

As the stories of Alba and GloFish show, whether people accept genetic engineering can sometimes have more to do with emotions, familiarity, and context than with any inherent or practical dangers in the technology itself or the animal. Most people aren't exposed to glowing mammals in research labs or in nature, which can make any glowing mammal seem "unnatural." But once we recover from the initial shock, it's worth considering: If people kept glowing bunnies as pets, what problems, if any, would that cause?

CHAPTER 13

DESIGNER DOGS, CUSTOM CATS & TEACUP PIGS

One day, a glowing green bunny may seem tame—even boring—compared to the made-to-order, novelty pets coming our way. How about a double-muscled guard dog? A cat-sized blue tiger? A faster racehorse? *A chickenosaurus?*

If someone somewhere can make it, someone somewhere will want it. After all, the pet industry has always used selective breeding to tinker with animals and create the coolest, most popular, most useful, and most convenient pets. That's business: promoting and selling a desirable product.

But traditional breeding practices have also led to genetic and inherited health problems, and animal welfare is probably the most important issue to consider with genetically engineered pets. No matter how bizarre the animals are, the main concern is, Will these animal companions be healthy, well cared for, and loved?

DESIGNER DOGS

The power of selective breeding to alter species is epitomized by the dog. Once wolves, dogs have been manipulated into about 170 recognized breeds that vary so radically in size and shape—from Chihuahuas to Great Danes, from basset hounds to greyhounds—they are like cartoon exaggerations.

Dogs didn't do this to themselves—people did it. We engineered, and continue to engineer, every canine feature, adjusting hair, ears, tail, height, length, muzzle, and even bark. The current "designer dog" craze epitomizes how much canine engineering people not only tolerate but desire.

The craze started in the 1980s when breeder Wally Conron created a nonallergenic guide dog for a client. After much trial and error, he crossed a poodle (which doesn't shed) with a Labrador retriever, creating the labradoodle. People loved it. Everyone wanted one. Tiger Woods, Jennifer Aniston, and Christie Brinkley eventually got one. Maybe you have one!

Labradoodles were originally bred in the 1980s as nonallergenic guide dogs. They became so wildly popular that they kick-started the "designer dog" craze that is still going strong today.

Since then the labradoodle's popularity has inspired breeders to mix poodles willy-nilly with many other dogs, making schnoodles (schnauzer + poodle), yorkiepoos (Yorkshire terrier + poodle), lhasapoos (Lhasa apso + poodle), doxiepoos (dachshund + poodle), dalmadoodles (dalmatian + poodle), and even more crosses: morkies (Maltese + Yorkshire terrier), puggles (beagle + pug), peke-a-pins (miniature pinscher + Pekingese), and so on.

But not all labradoodles and crosses turn out so well. When people breed for certain traits, dogs can sometimes develop genetically inherited health problems or defects. This is especially an issue with purebred dogs. They can develop health problems related to inbreeding. Elongated dachshunds get back problems; bulldogs have such massive heads, mothers can need C-sections to give birth; and flat-faced boxers can have trouble breathing. This is why many say the healthiest dogs are mutts, or random mixed breeds, since this increases genetic diversity.

"I opened a Pandora's box," Conron says. "I released a Frankenstein. So many people are just breeding for the money. So many of these dogs have physical problems, and a lot of them are just crazy."

Conron regrets what he started, but not everyone agrees. Many people love their labradoodles, and many of these dogs are healthy and happy. Conron's main concern is unscrupulous breeders, those who value looks and profit over the welfare of animals. He laments, "There are a few ethical breeders, but very, very few."

For instance, not every cross acquires the attributes breeders seek. Not every labradoodle inherits the poodle's nonshedding, "nonallergenic" trait. Not all are born healthy—both disease- and defect-free. But breeders might make these claims to make a sale.

This question of trust will be increasingly important as gene-edited pets become legalized and popular. Some people suggest genetically altering dogs to fix inherited health problems, though other kinds of genetic tinkering might cause new problems. This will mean revising regulations—for example, to ensure pet sellers state how pets were made and any problems owners might face.

One example is "double-muscled" animals. By removing or "knocking out" the myostatin gene, which regulates muscle growth, researchers have created beagles with double the amount of muscle.

These dogs were test cases to show that double muscling works. Double muscling can also be a naturally occurring mutation. Belgian Blue cattle, people, and whippets can also get it. By making double-muscled livestock, ranchers could produce animals with more meat, while bigger, stronger dogs might appeal to police and the military—or to anyone who wants the neighborhood's most intimidating guard dog. Yet double muscling creates difficult births (often requiring C-sections), and it might cause other physical ailments. These dogs might also be more dangerous to others.

CUSTOM CATS

Perhaps the holy grail of genetically engineered pets is the hypoallergenic cat. No one has successfully created one, but companies keep trying because there's a lot of money to be made. Lots of people love felines but literally can't live with them.

Researchers have discovered that cat allergies are probably a response to a single protein—Fel d 1, which helps cats maintain healthy skin. This protein might do other things, and male cats produce more than females. Scientists don't know what will happen to a cat if this protein is removed, but getting rid of it is the best, and maybe only, way to prevent human allergic reactions.

Over the years, several companies have sold what they swore were genetically altered, allergen-free cats, but these claims have always been false. While some cats produce less of an allergic reaction, all cats still produce some reaction—until the day a lab technician finally gets it right.

Like dogs, the traditional way people have altered cats is through selective breeding. This includes crossbreeding domestic cats with wild species, which has produced four recognized wild-domestic hybrids: the Savannah (part serval), the Bengal (part Asian leopard and Egyptian mau), the Serengeti (part Bengal and Oriental shorthair), and the Chausie (part wild jungle cat).

One hiccup with wild crossbreeds is that too much wildness makes for a difficult pet. Wolf dogs are the same. Several generations of cats must be bred to produce an animal tame enough to live with—yet this can lead to inherited health problems.

The Bengal cat is a domestic crossbreed that mixes the domestic Egyptian Mau and the wild Asian leopard cat. The original goal was to create a domestic cat with a leopard-like spotted and rosette-covered coat.

Still, one day, what was once fantasy may become reality: pint-sized, half-domesticated, glowing-pink tiger-cats will sit licking their paws and causing nary a sneeze.

MADE-TO-ORDER PETS

By the fourteenth century, people in China had bred the modern goldfish, and one contemporary Chinese company is going further: customers can preorder koi carp genetically designed to have the exact shape, colors, and patterning they want.

In Argentina, a biotech company is engineering double-muscled "super horses" that run faster. Under current rules, they could race in the Olympics.

Then there's the teacup pig.

Now a popular domestic pet, the Göttingen minipig (*shown*) was crossbred in Germany in the 1960s for research. Adults reach 60 to 75 pounds (27–34 kg). About twice as large, Vietnamese potbellied pigs grow to over 100 pounds (45+ kg) and are also popular pets.

In 2015, in a familiar story, scientists engineered a cloned micro pig that weighs only 30 pounds, or 14 kg (similar to an English cocker spaniel), because smaller pigs are easier for researchers to work with. Yet when the cute mini pigs were displayed at a science convention, everyone went *Awwww*, and the company thought: *Bingo! Let's sell it as a pet!*

The average farm pig weighs 1,000 pounds (454 kg), and potbellied pigs—which are popular pets—don't grow larger than 200 pounds (91 kg). As piglets, potbellied pigs are often misleadingly sold as "teacup pigs," but scientists now have the real deal: a tiny Babe even a child could hold.

But in 2017, the company scrapped its pet pig project. They didn't say why, but public resistance to genetic engineering is probably one reason. Like Alba the glowing bunny, a human-engineered teacup pig strikes many people as wrong, even though micro pigs appear to be healthy.

Like glowing animals, micro pigs are still being made. They just remain in labs and are used in research.

Public perceptions and outcry make a difference. They can influence what companies sell and don't sell. They can influence politicians and the laws we make. So with pets, where should we draw the line? If a genetically altered animal is acceptable for research, why can't the animal be kept as a pet, so long as the animal is healthy and tame? As for existing companion animals like dogs and cats, should we restrict genetic alterations in any way? For instance, does it make a difference if gene editing fixes problems we have (like allergies), fixes problems pets develop due to breeding practices (like inherited diseases), or if it simply creates harmless attributes we enjoy (like a different color)?

Ultimately, so long as companion animals are safe, healthy, cared for, and loved, does it matter what they look like or how they are made?

CHAPTER 14

[INSERT YOUR PET'S NAME HERE]

Pets are family, friends, and companions. We love them and share our lives with them. If they are service animals, we depend on them. So if we could restore these beloved friends after they die, would we?

That desire drives pet cloning.

But this raises an important philosophical question: What is the inner nature of a clone? Cloning creates a genetic physical copy, but does it reproduce a self, a mind, a soul?

One day, when the first human is cloned, maybe that person can tell us, but so far, the answer seems to be almost certainly no. All evidence suggests that a clone is a new animal with a new self. An original and a clone are more like twin siblings. They may look identical and share a remarkable number of traits and behaviors, but each has a unique personality.

"FERDINAND" GETS A SECOND CHANCE

Consider Chance, a Brahman bull that was the first steer ever cloned.

For fifteen years, Chance was a star attraction in Ralph Fisher's Photo Animals, a traveling menagerie of Texas longhorns, armadillos, buzzards, and exotic animals that Fisher brought to rodeos, state fairs, conventions, and corporate parties as entertainment.

Brahman bulls have epic backward-sweeping horns and aggressive reputations. They have a lot of inner aurochs. Not Chance. The white steer was perpetually sweet, docile, and kind. For hours, he patiently let Fisher pile children onto his massive back for keepsake photos. Chance liked to relax under a tree next to Fisher's house, "asked" to be brushed, loved to nuzzle, and would affectionately lick Fisher's boots. Fisher and his wife loved Chance as dearly as if he were their child. *This* Brahman was like Ferdinand come to life, the bull from the children's story who "liked to sit just quietly and smell the flowers."

In 1998 Chance died, and the Fishers made a radical decision: they asked researchers at Texas A&M University to clone Chance. In 1999, the clone was born, and Ralph named him Second Chance.

In this 2001 photo, Ralph Fisher greets Second Chance, the clone and physical spitting image of Fisher's gentle, beloved Brahman bull Chance, who died in 1998.

"I guess he's been reincarnated," Fisher told TV news reporters. He marveled at how Second Chance behaved exactly like Chance: lounging under the same tree, eating in the same manner, and acting just as tame.

Then, during Second Chance's fourth birthday party, the bull snapped, knocked Fisher to the ground, and attacked him. Fisher escaped without serious injury, and he blamed himself for the incident, thinking he must have accidentally triggered the bull. Fisher remained certain that Second Chance was Chance reborn, tame and kind. But two years later, it happened again. Out of the blue, Second Chance attacked, gored Fisher in the leg, and almost killed him.

Brahmans, Fisher said, are "like a light switch. That's why they use them as bucking bulls in rodeos. They get easily aggravated."

That's what made Chance so special. "Chance was one of those kinds of pets that are so rare—completely trustworthy with kids and grandkids," Fisher said. "That's why it was so hard for us to get it through our heads that Second Chance was not the same animal. It took me years, and a couple of hospital stays, to figure it out. . . . They looked the same, but there's something going on in that brain that's not the same. We learn by environment and life experiences, and there's something that the old guy got that this one didn't get."

THE BUSINESS OF CLONED PETS

It's a debate as old as time: What makes us who we are? Nature or nurture? Our genes or our upbringing and environment?

Clearly, both. Even with exactly the same genes, no two beings will ever be exactly the same.

The researchers at Texas A&M told Fisher this. They said cloning is reproduction, not reincarnation. But Fisher didn't want to believe it. He wanted Chance back.

This is what many people want when they clone their pets, even when they know better. In 2018 Barbra Streisand cloned her dog, Samantha, twice, creating Miss Violet and Miss Scarlet. She admitted that they have "different personalities," but "I'm waiting for them to get older so I can see if they have her brown eyes and her seriousness."

Sometimes, clones don't even look the same. The first cloned cat, CC, or Carbon Copy, was created in 2001. Ironically, the clone's fur patches didn't match the original. Calico coloring is determined randomly as the fetus develops, so even having the same genes doesn't always guarantee a "carbon copy."

Nevertheless, enough people are cloning pets and working animals to support cloning as a business. For those who aren't ready to commit, some companies offer the service of cryofreezing tissue samples of living pets so that should prices drop or technology improve, people can decide to clone those pets decades later.

ViaGen, which calls itself "America's most trusted animal cloning company," charges $35,000 to clone cats, $42,500 for horses, and $50,000 for dogs (since dogs are harder). That's expensive for a new pet. Most clients tend to be rich or interested in working animals. In 2013 and 2016, clones of top polo-playing horses won prestigious Argentine polo tournaments. Some people clone high-performing military and police dogs. Of course, cloned puppies need to be trained all over again, but one trainer said, "It does seem as if the cloned puppies are training at a higher success rate than conventionally bred litters." Cloned puppies start training younger and learn faster. That might mean that *some* of the original's inner talents remain.

THE COSTS OF CLONING

Cloning can't revive the dead—just like bioengineering can't undo extinction—so the decision to clone depends on what purpose it serves.

With livestock and working animals, what people want to reproduce, mostly, are the animal's physical qualities. Cloning is perfect for this. With pets, however, people usually want the whole package, body and soul—but that's impossible.

This makes pet cloning more controversial, since lots of other animals are needed to make one clone. Female animals provide eggs (which requires surgery), surrogate females carry the fertilized eggs to term (which requires an invasive procedure), and the majority of pregnancies aren't successful.

In 2005, to make the first cloned puppy, scientists extracted eggs from about 115 dogs, resulting in 1,095 embryos, which were inserted into 123 female dogs. This led to three births. Only one of those births was successful—Snuppy, which grew into a healthy dog. Despite improvements in technology, pregnancy rates for dogs still aren't higher than 40 percent, according to Sooam Biotech, the biggest South Korean pet cloning company.

The first cloned dog, named Snuppy, was created by the South Korean company Sooam Biotech in 2005. That same year, *Time* magazine dubbed Snuppy the "Invention of the Year."

Critics of pet cloning ask, Where do companies get all these other animals, and what happens to *them* afterward?

Companies are often vague about this. One practice is to use dogs and cats that were originally bred for research and to return them to those facilities. As bioethicist Jessica Pierce writes, "People who love their dog enough to clone her would likely shudder at the thought of this same dog being purpose-bred for use as a breeding machine."

Since cloning a pet is legal, whether to do it is a personal decision. As with so many situations in this book, each of us has to draw our own lines and make up our own minds.

CHAPTER 15

SPIDER GOATS, REMOTE-CONTROL ROACHES & RAT CYBORGS

We use animals for much more than companionship and food. Animals do all sorts of jobs for us and provide all sorts of products. Cattle pull plows, sheep provide wool, and horses carry us where cars can't. Pigeons once delivered messages, and dogs help detect bombs and rescue people.

With a little more tinkering, there's almost no end to what animals might do.

LIVING FACTORIES: SILKWORMS & SPIDER GOATS

One of the first living factories we ever created was the silkworm, which is actually the larva (caterpillar) form of a moth that spins silk. Over the centuries, to increase silk production, people altered this moth so completely, through breeding and upbringing, that it cannot live without us. It is too heavy to fly, won't run away, and won't even look for food if we don't feed it. It is as human-modified as any animal in this book.

In 1999, using genetic engineering for a similar purpose, a

For over 8,000 years, people have been harvesting silk from silkworms to make beautiful fabrics. Now, transgenic silkworms can produce BioSteel to make bulletproof vests, waterproof parkas, and food casings.

143

Montreal company created an entirely different "living factory"—the spider goat.

Ounce for ounce, spider silk is the strongest material in nature, stronger than steel. But it's hard to collect in useful amounts. People have tried to create spider farms, but when spiders get too crowded, they tend to eat one another. So researchers created transgenic goats that excrete spider silk proteins—from the golden orb weaver's dragline, to be precise—in their milk. Once the proteins are separated from the liquid, they can be spun into threads and combined to make BioSteel, which is superstrong, elastic, and biodegradable.

The company never developed a profitable product, however, and quit ten years later. Meanwhile, bioengineering animals to produce *human* proteins in their milk—to create disease-fighting medicines—has become an extremely profitable business (see chapter 16).

Recently, some companies have brought the spider goat back, along with new methods of producing spider silk proteins. These include creating transgenic silkworms or using synthetic biology (see page 116). Companies are also developing dozens of spider silk–based products.

Since the material is waterproof, North Face has made a parka out of it, and Adidas has made running shoes. Since it's unbelievably strong, companies are planning bulletproof vests, airbags, and artificial ligaments and tendons. Since, as a film or thin membrane, the material resists microbes, it makes an ideal casing for food—and one day might replace many plastics—or a protective coating on medical bandages, sutures, and catheters. It's already being used as "breathable skin protection" and "an antiwrinkle ingredient" in makeup.

As for the animals themselves, spider goats look, act, and live like goats—because that's what they are. They get milked often, which isn't unusual. Maybe the most troubling idea is that our sausages might soon come wrapped in material that originated in a spider's belly.

But hey—it's all-natural and environmentally friendly!

DIRTY JOBS: REMOTE-CONTROL ROACHES & BEETLE-BOTS

The military has long dreamed of using bugs as "bugs"—creating cyborg insects, outfitted with cameras and microphones, that can be controlled remotely and used for surveillance and spying.

That day is here.

These modified insects—most experiments use large beetles—can be used for more than *spying*. They can help find people trapped in earthquake-damaged buildings, enter broken pipes and sewers to find leaks, help survey tunnels and terrain, help find bombs, fly over your street and film people . . . oh wait, that's spying.

Most techniques for creating these robo-insects are mechanical, so they aren't technically examples of genetic engineering. Outfitted with tiny backpacks, with tiny electrodes attached to their tiny brains, beetle-bots move where we tell them to move: up, down, left, right, and so on. Another proposed method is to insert wires into the cocoons of larvae, so that as adult moths and insects develop, they emerge already wired!

This remote-controlled cockroach has electrodes connected to its antennae. This allows signals transmitted from the backpack to reach the roach's brain and control its movements.

But the latest techniques use optogenetics, which *does* require bioengineering. By modifying the nervous system of a dragonfly, pulses of light can be used to influence the insect. This is akin to mind control. The dragonfly still controls its own movements, but the light triggers responses in the brain that lead to the movements we want.

Want your own robo-roach? Backyard Brains sells "the world's first commercially available cyborg." The educational home kits come with everything you need to make one, but of course . . .

Cockroaches sold separately.

MIND CONTROL: RAT CYBORGS

Joking aside, controlling other creatures, even insects, raises ethical concerns. It's one thing to train animals to work for us—like search-and-rescue dogs—but it's entirely different to force them by hijacking their minds. Is it ever right to take over a being's thoughts?

We know insects experience pain. Inserting electrodes into an insect's brain, using light pulses to control its limbs, what must that feel like?

We may soon find out for ourselves.

Experiments with optogenetics are being conducted on mice. The technique works on any animal, and researchers are exploring whether and how it could be used with people—as a potential therapy for brain dysfunctions, such as epilepsy, sleep disorders, and Parkinson's disease. To work, genes related to photosynthesis in bacteria and plants are inserted into the subject's brain. Then, when certain lights flash, the subject—like a mouse or dragonfly—can be induced to wake up, fall asleep, become agitated, and move in specific ways.

Certainly, controlling a mind to heal it could be one good reason to do this.

An entirely different method of mind control uses a brain-to-brain interface. Brain-to-machine interfaces already exist. They are often used by people to control prosthetics and remote devices. But they also work the opposite way, so that a computer can control someone's brain.

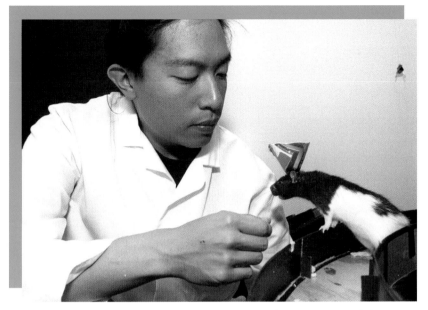

By attaching electrodes to a rat's brain, researchers can control the rat's movements to complete a maze.

Recent research on rats has shown that by linking devices wirelessly, a person can control a rat with their thoughts. That might involve guiding the animal through a maze simply by thinking, *left, right, left, left*. The "rat cyborg" has electrodes inserted in its brain, but the person just wears electrodes on the scalp.

These brain experiments reflect scientific curiosity. Researchers aren't sure how this technology might be used in the real world, but it evokes several scary, sci-fi scenarios—such as visions of remote-control, rat cyborg armies!

Researchers have raised another wild idea. If two people are hooked up together by a brain-to-brain interface, they might be able to directly experience each other's thoughts and feelings. If that works, imagine, for a moment, opening that same direct, two-way mental connection with mice, dogs, pigs, cows, ligers, mammephants, and any other animal we're tinkering with. What might we learn about how they feel?

BRAVE NEW US: IMPROVING HUMANS

In *Brave New World*, Aldous Huxley imagined a nightmare utopia, a world where people are custom designed for their jobs and engineered to be happy. Why be old, sick, or ugly when you can always be young, healthy, and beautiful? Why allow imperfection if perfection is possible?

All the genetic engineering we are doing with other animals can be done with ourselves. Human bodies operate by the same rules. We can edit genes, insert genes from other species, create human-animal chimeras, and even de-extinct lost human species like Neanderthals.

However, engineering humans is almost universally feared, condemned, and restricted. Almost no one wants to tinker with human embryos and bring genetically altered children into the world.

Almost.

In 2015 Chinese researchers genetically edited a nonviable human embryo, and in 2018 another Chinese researcher, He Jiankui, inserted a fertilized, gene-edited embryo in a woman who gave birth to twin girls.

These developments shocked the world. He was widely condemned for "reckless experimentation" that "shattered scientific, medical, and ethical norms." The Chinese government banned He from reproductive research and sentenced him to three years in jail.

Why did He do it? To engineer immunity to HIV. Preventing disease or fixing genetic defects is one purpose that many scientists agree would be morally acceptable . . . eventually—one day, once gene-editing technology improves and society is ready.

To become ready, we as a society need to discuss what's possible.

Like all animals, humans are constantly evolving and adapting to the environment; the modern world has changed people too. Over the last three centuries, the average human body size has increased 50 percent. Since 1900 the average human life span has almost doubled, from forty-four to eighty years. With genetic tinkering, we might increase longevity by repairing cellular damage due to aging. We might end genetic defects, develop personalized medicine, and bioengineer immunity to viruses. We might enhance intelligence and memory, using both bioengineering and bionics. We might enhance sensory perception, altering our eyes to see outside the color spectrum.

Right now, we could clone ourselves.

People propose we do some or all of this. Collectively, these ideas are known as transhumanism. Transhumanists ask, "Should we use science and technology to overcome death and become a far stronger species?"

One reason critics give for caution is our flawed human nature. People can be shortsighted, selfish, and unfair, and it's hard to write laws to avoid these things. For instance, some would say that treating disease would be justified, but not enhancing our abilities or "improving" humanity. Yet this line is fuzzy. Disease-resistance is certainly improvement.

Another distinction might be between germ line edits— or changing reproductive cells that create inheritable traits— and edits to somatic (or body) cells, which only affect the individual. Still, who gets to decide what is allowed? How do we avoid fostering inequality, so that the rich get these improvements (since they can afford them), while the poor do not? Most people are against the concept of eugenics, or creating an "ideal" human race, but does that mean individuals can't change themselves (or their children) to match their personal ideal?

One thing He Jiankui proved is that research doesn't necessarily stop while society debates. Two genetically altered girls already exist.

Now that we possess the power to guide our own evolution, how should we use it?

ANIMAL Rx: THE GOAT WILL SEE YOU NOW

Nothing embodies the promise and peril of genetic engineering as much as preventing and curing disease. The stakes don't get higher. Part 5 is about saving lives, and it explores how we're engineering animals to produce medicine, improve health, develop organs for transplant, and even, maybe, end certain diseases.

If we use biotechnology wisely, we could save countless lives. And not only human lives but the lives of many creatures.

Then again, as science fiction loves to remind us: technology can backfire. Just like a scalpel, the same tools that heal can hurt. At times, efforts to save lives will mean ending others. If we aren't careful, some attempts to save lives could go wrong and unleash death and disaster.

This only makes our decisions that much harder, since whatever we choose, lives hang in the balance.

CHAPTER 16

MEDICINAL GOATS & CHICKENS

magine a "healthy breakfast"—a tall glass of milk, a plate of bacon and eggs—in which the food also functions as medicine. It provides missing vitamins, contains less fat, and fights disease.

This is another main reason we are tinkering with farm animals: to improve human health. There are two basic approaches. One is to create transgenic animals, similar to spider goats, which produce beneficial proteins in their milk and eggs. Then we separate out those proteins to make other products—in this case, drugs.

The other approach is to directly consume the products of gene-edited animals—their meat, milk, and eggs.

Based on what you've read so far, which approach do you think is already widely accepted and used, and which is not?

PHARMING: LIVING DRUG FACTORIES

Using transgenic animals to help produce medicine has been dubbed "pharming," and every year, more "farmaceuticals" are approved for sale.

The human body produces proteins, enzymes, and antibodies that help prevent illness and fight disease. These are often the basis for powerful drugs that treat the most serious illnesses, like cancer, hemophilia, and diabetes. Yet producing these in bulk outside the human body is difficult and expensive. It's almost like trying to twist a BioSteel thread out of spiderwebs. But we can engineer almost any farm animal to produce human proteins and enzymes by the bucketful.

In 2009 the first "transgenic animal drug" to be approved in the United States was ATryn. This anticoagulant drug prevents or "melts" blood clots, which can be life-threatening. Our livers make anticoagulant naturally, but as many as one in two thousand people are born without this ability. For them, taking an anticoagulant is essential.

These genetically modified chickens are being bred to produce eggs that contain a special protein, which is used in drugs to treat cancer.

Since then the milk of transgenic rabbits, sheep, goats, cattle, and camels and the eggs of transgenic chickens have been turned into drugs that treat skin cancer, cholesterol, AIDS, Alzheimer's, heart disease, and more.

Best of all, this process is inexpensive and doesn't seem to harm the animals. Studies of transgenic chickens show "no adverse effects on the chickens themselves, which lay eggs as normal."

Professor Harry Griffin—the director of Scotland's Roslin Institute, which cloned Dolly the sheep—has said that flocks of transgenic hens "can produce in bulk, they can produce cheaply, and indeed, the raw material for this production system is quite literally chicken feed."

As a result, the millions of transgenic animals serving the biotech drug industry could be one of the most beneficial uses of genetic engineering—saving human lives without harming the animals that are doing the saving.

GOT (TRANSGENIC GOAT) MILK?

Common illnesses can also be deadly, especially in poor communities without reliable access to modern medicine, proper sanitation, adequate diets, and clean water. For instance, diarrhea is the world's second-leading cause of death for children under five, and diarrheal disease kills about 437,000 children every year.

Diarrheal disease is easily preventable. For children, the simplest prevention method is breastfeeding. Human breast milk contains a high abundance of lysozyme, a natural "wonder drug" that boosts a child's immune system, fights bacteria, and promotes a healthier digestive system. All mammals produce milk with some lysozyme, but human milk can have up to three thousand times more than other animal milk has. Infant formula has barely any.

In the 1990s, two University of California at Davis professors, James Murray and Elizabeth Maga, created transgenic goats that produce a thousand times more lysozyme than regular goats. They tested the transgenic milk on pigs and found that it significantly improved the disease-fighting health of the pigs' digestive systems. They also found that it was safe to consume and that the lysozyme was more effective when drunk as milk rather than taken as a purified supplement.

They sought FDA approval and were denied, so they moved some goats to Brazil, where diarrhea is an ongoing threat. There, they still couldn't win government approval.

"Every human in the world eats lysozyme every day of their life," Murray has said. "It's clearly not an allergen and it's clearly not toxic."

In the late 2010s, their research grants ran out, and they couldn't find anyone to provide more funding. "At present, we are on hold," Murray says. Until more funding arrives, the potentially lifesaving goats bleat in fenced pens, being goats, while over the last two decades, perhaps millions of children might still be alive if they'd had access to their milk.

Transgenic goats such as this one were created at the University of California at Davis to produce increased lysozyme in their milk. Lysozyme, an antibacterial enzyme, is abundant in human breast milk and helps prevent intestinal infections and diarrhea in infants.

Other, similar efforts include hypoallergenic chicken eggs. Worldwide, about 2 percent of children are allergic to eggs. Not only can't they eat omelets, but they can't have many normal vaccines (which are produced using chicken eggs).

However, Timothy Doran, a molecular biologist in Australia, is using CRISPR on chickens to alter the genes that produce the proteins that cause this allergic reaction. Doran's daughter, who is allergic, inspired him to solve this problem, and if the gene-edited eggs ever get approved, he said, "I've got someone ready and waiting to try the first egg."

Researchers have been trying to create a "low-fat pig" since the 1980s. Bacon that's good for you? Well, *better* for you.

In 2004 scientists created a transgenic pig by adding an enzyme from a nematode worm, which converts a pig's normally unhealthy, omega-6 fatty acids into good-for-us omega-3 acids. Found in fish oils, omega-3 acids seem to lower the risk of heart disease and are used to combat the symptoms of attention deficit hyperactivity disorder (ADHD) and other conditions.

As you've likely guessed, the "healthy breakfast" described above doesn't exist—at least not yet. Like all the genetically engineered food animals in part 3 (except for clones, AquAdvantage salmon, and the GalSafe pig), none of these animals have been approved for human consumption.

UNHEALTHY FEAR: REGULATION & GOLDEN RICE

Another example of a lifesaving GM food is golden rice. This is rice modified with enhanced vitamin A. Vitamin A deficiency is a major cause of blindness for children in impoverished communities, where malnutrition is rampant. It causes perhaps a half million kids to go blind annually. Like lysozyme-enhanced goats, golden rice was first developed nearly two decades ago, but due to strict government regulations, it was only approved for consumption in 2019.

Biology writer Ed Regis calls this delayed approval "a modern tragedy"—since so many children might have avoided blindness except for the "irrational fears of GMOs, ignorance of the science involved, and overzealous adherence to the precautionary principle."

As these and other stories show, public attitudes, government regulations, and money can combine to either block or allow the use of genetically modified and transgenic animals. As a society, we have approved of transgenic goats if they help us *make* medicine—or other products such as BioSteel—but so far we have rejected and resisted consuming them as medicine or food by drinking their milk.

As with genetically modified plants, governments, research institutions, and companies act in part based on what they think people will accept. If people refuse to drink GM milk from transgenic animals—for *any* reason—then why fund research and go through the expensive, time-consuming effort to get regulatory approval? Even if approved, no one will buy or consume this product.

But people who are suffering and dying from conditions that could be treated by modified milk or eggs might want that option. Who benefits might be another reason for the differences in attitudes, funding, and approval of GM animals in medicine.

Lysozyme goats and golden rice are inexpensive solutions for health problems related to poverty. In poor nations, diarrheal disease and vitamin A deficiency are urgent and widespread issues. In rich countries like the United States, despite the presence of poverty, no one is going to make a lot of money selling lysozyme goats, and few Americans truly need them. But many people in all countries need anticoagulant drugs and other "farmaceuticals," and the multibillion-dollar biotech industry is making tons of money developing these.

So, the reason lysozyme goat milk hasn't been approved isn't because it's unsafe to drink or ineffective against diarrheal disease. It's because academic researchers don't have the resources to *prove* it's safe to the satisfaction of current regulations. Multinational biotech companies have little incentive to develop products that won't be very profitable. And many people still fear consuming any animal or animal product created with the tools of genetic engineering, even when those animals save lives.

CHAPTER 17

MOSQUITOES AGAINST MALARIA

Mosquito-borne diseases are a global scourge. Their very names inspire fear: malaria, yellow fever, dengue fever, West Nile virus, Zika, Ebola.

Every year, on average, malaria infects two hundred million people and kills half a million. Dengue fever infects three hundred ninety million people and kills twenty-five thousand. Because people travel everywhere, viruses can spread like wildfire. By 2010 Zika had occurred in a few regions. By 2016 it had exploded into a worldwide pandemic, appearing on every continent and in over eighty countries.

But, using genetic engineering, we can theoretically end these plagues.

MOSQUITO VERSUS MOSQUITO: STOPPING THE PLAGUE

Traditional methods of controlling insects are inadequate. They help, but they are not enough to stop mosquitoes, especially the *Aedes aegypti* mosquito, the real plague carrier for humans. This species has evolved to live in human environments, thriving in yards and dumps, and it's never been more numerous.

Using CRISPR, we could genetically alter mosquitoes in several ways to stop the spread of disease or even to wipe out this mosquito entirely. The most radical proposals use a gene drive—a genetic edit to reproductive cells (or germ cells) that ensures that the edited gene will be inherited by virtually all offspring. Gene drives only work effectively in species that reproduce quickly—particularly insects and certain rodents—but in those species, it can potentially spread through the entire population.

For *Aedes aegypti* mosquitoes, one proposed gene drive could pass a malaria-resistance gene to virtually all subsequent generations. Or a gene drive could pass along a change that sterilizes all female mosquitoes or that forces females to produce only male offspring

These genetically modified mosquitoes were created by Oxitec and released in Brazil in 2015 to slow the spread of dengue fever.

(which do not bite). Either of those options could eventually drive that species to extinction.

Overall, of the thirty-five hundred known species of mosquitoes, only a hundred seek human blood. Of those, only a few dozen are responsible for spreading most human diseases. So the question society must answer is, Is it okay to snuff out a few mosquito species to stop malaria forever—or is "specicide" going too far?

Oxitec has been testing both genetically altered mosquitoes and public acceptance. Since 2013 the company has conducted several pilot programs in Malaysia, the Cayman Islands, and Brazil. Each time, mosquito populations have dropped by more than 90 percent. In 2020 one Brazilian city, Indaiatuba, agreed to expand the program. In 2020, after years of opposition by locals and environmental advocates, Oxitec won EPA and community approval for the first pilot program in the United States, in the Florida Keys, from 2021 to 2022.

There are other methods besides engineering mosquito extinctions. The World Mosquito Program inserts a particular bacterium into mosquitoes that prevents diseases like dengue fever from spreading to people. The mosquitoes spread the beneficial bacteria among themselves as they breed, but it doesn't kill the virus or eliminate the mosquitoes. As of 2021, the World Mosquito Program had projects in eleven countries.

We could also use gene drives with other insects, such as to modify or eliminate the ticks that spread Lyme disease and the agricultural pests that destroy crops.

RAT VERSUS RAT: ELIMINATING INVASIVE SPECIES

Gene drives can also be used with fast-reproducing mammals such as rodents.

In contemporary society, rats and other rodents are an invasive species that can disrupt and destroy ecosystems. Particularly on islands, nonnative, invasive rodents often have no natural predators. As their own populations explode, they can drive many native species to death's door.

Who spread these rodents around? We did.

Rodents typically hitch a ride to islands on human vehicles—think planes, trains, automobiles, and boats—and this has become a widespread problem. Some people estimate that 90 percent of the world's islands have become infested with nonnative rodents. This is one reason why islands are home to 40 percent of all endangered species and why island species make up 80 percent of all known extinctions.

With gene drives, we might fix this problem. Island by island, we could engineer nonnative female rats or mice so they birthed only males. Within a few generations, unable to find a mate all those lonely males would die—and the remaining island species and their ecosystems might recover.

FROGS, FERRETS & ELEPHANTS: PREVENTING WILDLIFE DISEASE

Infectious diseases don't only affect people. Virulent plagues threaten other animals too, and we could use genetic engineering to help these species survive.

Black-footed ferrets and prairie dogs suffer from the sylvatic plague. Spread by fleas, this is the same bacteria that causes the bubonic plague in humans. But we could genetically modify each species to resist the disease or the parasites that carry it.

Chytrid fungus is decimating populations of frogs, and white-nose syndrome is harming bats, but we could modify each fungus so that it causes sickness but not death. This would help these animals evolve their own disease resistance. A virus in Asian elephants kills calves, and avian malaria—also spread by mosquitoes—exacts its terrible price among Hawaii's native birds.

White-nose syndrome in bats and chytrid fungus in frogs are deadly plagues, but through genetic engineering, scientists could modify both the fungus and the animals to help these species survive.

Which raises the question, If we already have the power to stop these diseases, to save ourselves and other species, why aren't we doing it?

THE DOOMSDAY SCENARIO

If we want to destroy insects, we don't need gene drives. The poison DDT is an extremely effective pesticide. In the United States, DDT was widely used in the 1940s and 1950s, until we realized that DDT poisons everything—birds, fish, crops, us. The blind destruction caused by DDT helped spark the modern environmental movement, and DDT is now banned in many countries.

We know firsthand that extreme solutions can have extreme consequences. With gene drives, things could go very badly, very quickly.

One concern is evolution. If a gene drive or genetic change isn't 100 percent effective, it might create a monster that is worse than the original. Unaffected mosquitoes might develop resistance to the gene drive and spread that resistance to other mosquitoes. Or a virus could adapt and develop into an unstoppable "super virus." In fact, before DDT was banned, some mosquitoes started developing resistance to it.

After a 2015 trial release of altered mosquitoes in Brazil, a controversial 2019 study of the remaining mosquito populations found that some offspring of the altered mosquitoes had survived and successfully mated with wild females. Oxitec, which made the mosquitoes, admitted that its research showed up to 3 percent of offspring survived. What wasn't and still isn't known is whether these survivors were "more robust" hybrids and thus more dangerous to people. That is the doomsday scenario people fear: that bioengineering might accidentally create *stronger* mosquitoes.

Another concern is how to stop gene drives from "jumping" to other species. For example, a gene drive that's designed to eliminate only the *Aedes aegypti* mosquito could get accidentally passed along to other mosquito species or even to all thirty-five hundred. If this happened, in theory, all mosquitoes in a region or a continent (or on Earth) could disappear. We have no idea what havoc that might cause. Like all species, mosquitoes play a beneficial role in nature (for instance, as pollinators).

Similarly, on islands, if gene-drive rats escaped (in the exact same way rodents often arrive, as stowaways on human vessels), they might pass that gene drive to rats everywhere. Modified insects and animals could crossbreed with related species we value. Not all rodents are "pests." As we know from red wolves and polar bears, population declines and environmental pressures can drive species to mate with distant relatives for survival.

Perhaps the biggest fear is bioterrorism. As with synthetic biology, gene drives could be used as weapons, much like chemical warfare. People could revise animals so they transmitted diseases, not eliminated them.

This is why researchers—from the US military to geneticists like George Church—are also exploring "reverse gene drives." In an emergency—after an accident, a test gone wrong, or a deliberate attack—these could be created and released to undo the original genetic change.

This is why we hesitate. Gene drives have been called an extinction technology because they affect entire species. It's a genetic cure that could be worse than the disease. Gene drives embody the awesome potential of genetic engineering, but they also represent why many people fear anything to do with it.

As the science writer Bryan Walsh said, with biotechnology, "it has become increasingly difficult to draw a distinction between research that benefits humankind and work that could lead to our extinction."

CHAPTER 18

PIGS WITH HUMAN HEARTS

A nother way genetically engineered animals may save lives and improve human health is by providing organs for transplant.

Organ shortages are an urgent worldwide problem. In America every year, more than a hundred thousand people are on organ waiting lists but only a third receive transplants. Meanwhile, every day, about twenty people die waiting. In China, perhaps three times that many people are on waiting lists.

Naturally, most people—probably *all* people—prefer human organ donation, but there aren't enough human donors. So, for decades, scientists have been trying to figure out how to use organs from other animals, a procedure called xenotransplantation.

The most famous animal organ transplant occurred in 1984, when Baby Fae, a newborn girl, received a baboon's heart. The surgery was successful, but Baby Fae only lived another twenty days. In the 1990s,

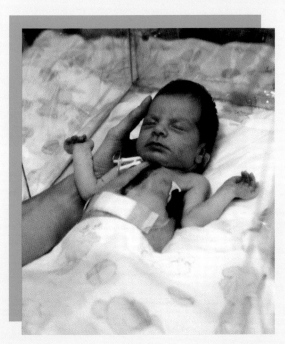

Stephanie Fae Beauclair, who became known as "Baby Fae," received a baboon heart transplant on October 26, 1984, to replace her own failing heart. She passed away twenty days later on November 15.

two people received baboon livers and six people received baboon kidneys, but no one lived longer than two months.

The problem with xenotransplantation is organ rejection. The human immune system attacks foreign organs as invaders, the same way it attacks disease. Researchers currently hope to solve this problem by genetically engineering animals to grow organs that the human body will accept.

Like gene drives, this effort raises some of the most difficult and unsettling questions about genetic engineering.

XENOTRANSPLANTATION: PIGS, PROTEINS & PATHOGENS

For several reasons, pigs have become preferred for xenotransplantation. Their organs are human-sized, their immune systems are similar, and they are abundant. We already raise billions for food and medical research. In theory, it shouldn't make a difference if we engineer some to harvest their organs, right?

Two approaches are being tried.

One is to genetically edit cloned pig embryos using CRISPR to disrupt or stop the production of various pig proteins that trigger human antibodies. These pig proteins lead to organ rejection by the human immune system. But transplanting pig organs also carries a different risk: the pig organ might also make a person sick by transmitting an infectious pathogen or retrovirus. This could kill the person even if the body accepts the transplant. To avoid this, the pig's genome must also be edited to eliminate any pathogen-causing DNA.

This complex genetic work is nearly finished. If it's successful, the same might be done with sheep and cows.

Scientists *already* believe they have bioengineered a potentially safer, nonantibody-triggering, nonpathogen-causing pig heart. In several trials, scientists have transplanted these modified pig hearts into baboons. Since primates are our nearest relatives, they provide the best

These five cloned piglets were created in 2002 by PPL Therapeutics, which created Dolly the sheep, in order to develop organs suitable for human transplant.

test for whether a transplant will work in humans. In a 2020 study, the majority of baboons that received transplants showed "prolonged survival," or living without complications for at least three months, and two lived for six months before they were terminated. In a 2016 study, several baboons with transplants lived for over a year.

These results mean "that it now looks as though pig-to-human heart transplantation is feasible," one researcher said. The next step is testing people. Once appropriate human candidates are identified and selected, human trials might begin in 2022.

When this happens, it won't be the first pig-to-human tissue transplant. That occurred in 2019 when living skin from a genetically altered pig was grafted onto a person to help heal serious burn wounds. Further trials have shown no safety issues or adverse effects from the pig grafts, called Xeno-Skin. One scientist said this "will pave the way for other types of transplantations, like kidneys, hearts, lungs, or livers."

Then an even more significant breakthrough occurred in September 2021. In a first-of-its-kind experiment, doctors externally attached a genetically modified pig kidney (from a GalSafe pig; see page 115) to the blood vessels in the leg of a comatose patient, who was being kept alive on a ventilator. The patient's family approved the procedure, which lasted for two days, during which the kidney functioned normally without any signs of organ rejection.

Dr. Robert Montgomery, who performed the procedure at NYU Langone Transplant Institute, said, "It was better than I think we even expected. It just looked like any transplant I've ever done with a living donor."

While it still might be years before these modified pig kidneys will be approved for internal transplants in living patients, that day is on the horizon.

For internal organs, the second approach being tried is to modify a pig embryo so it grows a genetically human organ. The technique is called interspecies blastocyst complementation. This scientific word salad boils down to making a part-pig, part-human animal, a genuine chimera.

This involves putting human stem cells into a pig embryo—specifically one in which the genes for making a particular organ have been disabled. In theory, the human cells will take over and make this organ. Since the organ would be composed mostly or entirely of human cells, a person's immune system probably wouldn't reject it. If transplant patients used their own cells, this would be like regrowing their own organ in another animal.

In 2017 this technique was tested successfully on rodents, when rat-mouse chimeras were induced to grow organs of either species.

Here's the it-used-to-be-science-fiction-but-now-it's-real worry: What if, during this process, chimera pigs were humanized by accident in other ways? For instance, the human stem cells—which can become any type of cell—might influence brain development or merge with the reproductive organs. If either of these happened, it's theoretically possible that this human-pig chimera might think more like a human or be able to give birth to a new part-human pig.

These nightmare scenarios evoke the human-animal hybrids in *The Island of Dr. Moreau.* That's why transplant researchers are, *ahem*, continuing to tinker to make sure this doesn't happen.

MONKEYS, MEDICINE & MINDS

One unsettling question these efforts raise is whether certain species like primates are already too much like us to be used and experimented on in these ways.

The use of monkeys and apes in research is controversial. Not only are their genetics very similar to ours, their minds can be as well. Nearly all scientists agree that the four great apes—chimpanzees, bonobos, gorillas, and orangutans—can feel pain and suffer and have self-awareness similar to humans.

For this reason, most countries have some kind of restriction on using primates in research. In 1999 New Zealand was the first nation to ban the use of great apes, and more countries have followed with similar or partial research restrictions. The United States allows research on monkeys (including baboons) but currently bans federal funding of human-animal chimeras.

This issue is about more than "animal welfare," or how we care for animals. Some groups, like the Nonhuman Rights Project, believe we should grant certain species legal rights, including the right to liberty, or freedom from imprisonment, and the right to "bodily integrity," or freedom from physical abuse and experimentation. Whether nonhuman animals are eligible for any right under the law depends on whether we consider them "persons." The terms *human* and *person* are not the same. *Human* refers to our species, which is primarily (but not exclusively) defined by our genetics, while *person* is a legal term referring to an individual who possesses moral and legal rights. All humans are considered persons, but must all persons be human?

Candidate species for nonhuman personhood include all the great apes, elephants, dolphins, whales, and perhaps others. Some countries have begun doing this. In 2016 Argentina recognized an individual chimpanzee as a "person" under the law.

As bioethicist John Loike has written, "How we define human status and apply personhood to any organism underscores a central tenet of bioethics and social justice—respecting the quality and value of life." This applies to any animal, but it's particularly important in medical research, which regularly justifies sacrificing animals to save human lives. As a new type of being, human-animal

In 2019, Chinese scientists genetically modified a macaque to develop a circadian rhythm disorder in order to study how this condition impacts mental health. In a controversial first, they then cloned the monkey five times so that all five cloned macaques (*shown*) possessed the disorder.

chimeras will test both our legal and ethical concepts.

For instance, when it comes to organ transplantation, it would actually be more efficient to genetically modify baboon organs, not pig organs. And an international team, working in China, is currently researching how to create human-monkey chimeras for transplants. In 2019 they announced the creation of human-monkey embryo cells, but they halted growth after a few weeks, since they don't know yet how to stop these chimeras from becoming *too* human.

Some researchers, however, actually *do* want to bioengineer animals, like pigs and monkeys, in more humanlike ways. If pigs possessed human brain cells and thought more like us, it might improve studies of brain disorders (such as Parkinson's disease). If monkeys were created with human reproductive cells, it could aid the study of human infertility issues.

It almost sounds like *Rise of the Planet of the Apes* come to life: in the name of medical research and curing human disease, some scientists might genetically engineer humanized beings that, either legally or morally, might qualify as "persons" with the right not to be used in research.

This is the slippery slope of genetic engineering and our current technology. One minute we're trying to solve the human transplant crisis, and the next we're facing a host of disturbing dilemmas: about using animals in research, human-animal chimeras, pigs and monkeys with more human minds, and even whether to genetically modify humans to prevent the diseases that require transplants.

Still, biotechnology could potentially sidestep the ethical knots of xenotransplantation. Using either stem cells or 3D bioprinting, we might make lab-grown organs separate from a body. Smaller organoids have already been created of livers, stomachs, and even brains to study disease, so we might one day make organs for patients from their own cells without involving other animals at all.

BLURRED LINES & DIFFICULT CHOICES

Human-animal chimeras and hybrids used to be the stuff of novels, movies, and the occasional mad scientist. In the 1920s a Soviet researcher tried to impregnate female chimpanzees with human sperm, but he was arrested before any "humanzees" were born. Authors Mary Shelley and H. G. Wells both imagined fictional beings that are human in mind but different in body. These imagined altered creatures, part us and part not, blur the line of what is human.

With genetic engineering, we can create such creatures—in several ways—and sane, smart, concerned scientists *want to* for perhaps the most valid, urgent reason: saving human lives.

Given what we *can* do, what *should* we do?

We need to decide where to draw the line: Is it OK to modify animal bodies to contain genetically human organs but only if animal minds are not changed, even by accident? Or is altering animal minds OK but only if the goal is saving human lives? Is it OK to use primates to create or test modified organs for transplant, or should baboons never be used in medical research? Is using pigs for transplants OK, since we eat them as food, or is altering them to harvest their organs going too far? Or should we avoid all human-animal chimeras of any kind for any reason?

These issues lead to even more profound questions about the nature of life and our responsibility to others. What truly distinguishes being human—our genes or our minds? How similar are the minds of humans and animals already? How does *any* creature deserve to be treated?

Just because these are difficult questions, however, doesn't mean we shouldn't try to answer them. People have always asked these questions. If anything, genetic engineering only makes them more important.

As we make new animals and as we blur lines between species—and perhaps even modify our own species—we need to consider our values, concepts, definitions, and laws. Ideally, we can write laws that align with what most people find morally acceptable, and we can devise regulations that embody reasonable caution, not unfounded fears. Then we can pursue the practical, safe solutions that genetic engineering makes possible.

When decisions are complex and overwhelming, it can help to simplify the question. For any genetic-engineering project, we might ask, What decision will cause the least harm and be the most compassionate for everyone?

In *Frankenstein* and *The Island of Dr. Moreau*, the doctors in these stories become the real villains because their lack of compassion and irresponsible choices hurt the very beings they create.

In the end, we might not be able to answer every question that genetic engineering raises. We won't fix every problem. Sometimes, we will make mistakes, and new technology will certainly come along, revise what's possible, and force us to reconsider what to do all over again.

So long as we pledge to take care of all beings, including ourselves, as best we can—no matter how we use genetic technologies or what we call animals—we will hopefully make the best choices.

AUTHOR'S NOTE

The idea for this book arose as I was writing *Last of the Giants*, a YA book on conservation that focuses on recently extinct and critically endangered animals. I thought that book was about endings, but with several species—aurochs, passenger pigeons, rhinos—I had to include a strange caveat: *But wait! These stories aren't over. Genetic engineers are trying to bring these animals back . . .*

As I went down the rabbit hole of bioengineering, I felt a need to tell this story, which is of new beginnings and a future filled with long-imagined, once-mythical creatures built by us.

Despite this weird, controversial topic, Hallie Warshaw and Dan Harmon were supportive and encouraging from the beginning, and without Hallie, this book would not exist. She brought me along when Zest Books moved to Lerner Publishing, and Lerner has been just as welcoming.

I'm grateful to the entire Lerner team, but especially to Ashley Kuehl, who first took on this project; Shaina Olmanson, who shepherded it to publication; Quinton Singer, whose thoughtful editing improved the book immensely; and assistant editor Jesseca Fusco. Nor can I imagine this book or these animals without the wondrous illustrations of Greer Stothers.

A bevy of knowledgeable readers helped me keep my facts and terms straight, but make no mistake: any and all errors are mine, as are the views expressed, and neither should reflect on those who graciously gave me feedback.

I am particular indebted to two animal geneticists at the University of California, Davis: James Murray and Alison Van Eenennaam. Both are leading researchers and pioneers who read portions of this manuscript; their projects appear in these pages.

A number of high school and middle school teachers also commented on early drafts: Anthony Danese and Joseph Componile at Morristown High School; Catherine Rosenthal at Gottesman RTW Academy; and Michael Locher, Bailey Batty, and Bruce Rubin at Pioneer Valley Chinese Immersion Charter School. I'm especially thankful to Bruce, my brother-in-law, for his enthusiasm.

I will forever be grateful to animal ethicist Marc Bekoff; our work together on his books originally opened my eyes to the wild, wonderful inner lives of animals and to our responsibility toward them.

Most of all, I would be nothing without my family. My children, Jackson and Miranda, still listen patiently and hardly ever roll their eyes when I go on and on about some new animal, and my wife, Deanna, is patience personified. Her encouragement, support, and love mean the world to me.

GLOSSARY

artificial insemination: to insert sperm directly into a uterus or cervix to assist with conception

assisted reproductive technology: with livestock, any reproductive technique that handles or modifies eggs, sperm, embryos, or more than one of these

back-breeding: a type of selective breeding whose goal is to re-create the traits of an extinct ancestor species in a new animal

bioengineering: using gene editing to alter an organism; applying engineering principles to biology, especially in medicine; in USDA food guidelines, "detectable genetic material that has been modified through certain lab techniques and cannot be created through conventional breeding or found in nature"; also called genetic engineering

biological species concept: one taxonomic method for defining animal species; any population in which individuals mate in the wild and give birth to fertile offspring

breed: usually used for domestic animals; a subgroup or type within a species (like a subspecies) with shared characteristics and common ancestors and capable of mating with other breeds

chimera: a bioengineered animal that contains genetically distinct cells from two or more different species (this differs from hybrid, transgenic, or GM animals, in which every cell contains the same genetic alteration); in mythology, a creature that is part lion, part goat, and part serpent

clone: an animal that is an identical genetic copy of another animal

CRISPR-Cas9: CRISPR (clustered regularly interspaced short palindromic repeats) is a programmable gene-editing tool that uses an immune-system enzyme (Cas9) to find, delete, add, and/or modify specific genes or DNA sequences

crossbreeding: in animals, when two different species, subspecies, or breeds mate and produce offspring

cryobanking: to store living tissue, cells, and genetic material using cryopreservation, or freezing at extremely low temperatures

de-extinction: the use of bioengineering to clone, reproduce, or create a genetic and physical replica of an extinct species

DNA: a self-replicating molecule found in every cell that carries an organism's entire genetic information (its *genome*), or the instructions to develop and reproduce; it stands for deoxyribonucleic acid

ectogenesis: to develop embryos in an artificial womb or outside an animal's uterus

epigenetics: the study of gene expression (or epigenesis), or how environmental factors (and other genes) influence and guide the way genes instruct an organism's development; changes to gene expression can lead the same genes to create different physical, heritable traits

evolution: the process by which generations of living organisms diversify or change into different species, such as when mating, environmental changes, and/or behavioral adaptions cause inherited changes to genes or gene expression

evolutionary developmental biology: to study embryo development to determine how organisms evolved from or relate to ancestral species; also called evo-devo

extinction: when all members of a species no longer exist

functionally extinct: when the only remaining members of a species live in captivity

gene: a specific sequence of DNA that produces or influences one or more inherited traits by providing instructions for the creation of proteins and controlling the expression of other genes

gene drive: any genetic edit to reproductive cells (or germ cells) that guarantees that the genetic changes will be inherited by virtually all offspring

gene editing: any technique that alters, removes, or adds specific genes (or DNA sequences) in a genome

genetically modified: usually refers to any deliberate genetic change to an organism by any method or technique but also sometimes defined in specific ways for food regulations; also genetically modified organism (GMO)

genetic engineering: deliberate manipulation of an organism's genome by any method

genome: the complete set of genes or genetic material in an organism; every cell contains an organism's entire genome

germ cells: reproductive cells (sperm and eggs, known as gametes) that combine to form a zygote, or fertilized egg; genetic edits to germ cells (germ line edits) are inherited by offspring

hybrid: in animals, the offspring of two different species (offspring between subspecies or breeds are usually not called hybrids)

introgression: when two species crossbreed and create a fertile hybrid, and the hybrid offspring breeds back with either parent species, so that some genes are shared and retained between the two parent species

in vitro fertilization: to fertilize eggs outside the body and then implant the embryo in a womb

optogenetics: a technique that uses pulses of light to control neurons in the brain, ones that have been genetically modified to respond to that light

portmanteau: a word or animal name that is a blend of two other words; traditionally, animal portmanteaus start with the name of the male species and end with the female

precautionary principle: a decision-making approach that proposes using caution when the negative impacts or effects of actions are uncertain. In genetic engineering, it most often refers to not using, eating, or releasing a genetically modified organism until it has been studied and determined safe.

recombinant DNA: DNA that is a combination of genes from different species (one type of transgenesis)

selective breeding: deliberately breeding particular animals to develop desirable traits in a population, breed, or species

sequencing: deciphering or reading the exact order of DNA in a gene or genome

somatic cell: any specialized body cell in an organism or any cell that can form only one type of body part and is not a reproductive cell

somatic cell nuclear transfer: a method used for cloning that takes the nucleus from an adult somatic cell and inserts it into the egg cell of another animal

species: in animal taxonomy, a group of animals sharing common attributes and capable of producing fertile offspring; many criteria are used to define and group species, and dozens of different "species concepts" exist

stem cells: unspecialized reproductive cells that can become specialized somatic cells to form parts of the body. Multipotent stem cells can become a limited number of cell types, pluripotent stem cells can become any cell type, and induced pluripotent stem cells are adult somatic cells reprogrammed to become pluripotent stem cells.

subspecies: in animal taxonomy, a subgroup within a species that is capable of mating with others of that species. Subspecies are often defined by geography (or as isolated populations) but also by different traits, genes, and so on.

synthetic biology: the creation of novel DNA or gene sequences in new or artificial combinations; often used to refer to engineering novel organisms or redesigning natural ones for specific applications

taxonomy: any classification system; for animals, the system of naming and defining species (and the extended relationships among all species)

transgenesis: inserting new genes or DNA sequences into an animal's genome; transgenic engineering includes inserting "foreign" genes from one species into another species as well as creating new genes (or DNA sequences) using the species' own DNA; either process creates a transgenic animal

transhumanism: the belief that humans can improve their species through biotechnology and other means; both a general term and the name of a philosophical movement

unextinct: an animal created by de-extinction

xenotransplantation: to transplant the organs or tissue from one species into another species (creating a chimera)

SOURCE NOTES

11 "[Humans] are like . . . an ice age.": Owen Gaffney and Will Steffen, "Introducing the Terrifying Mathematics of the Anthropocene," *Conversation*, February 10, 2017, https:// theconversation.com/introducing the-terrifying-mathematics-of-the -anthropocene-70749.

11 "We are living . . . human-free nature.": Chris D. Thomas, *Inheritors of the Earth: How Nature Is Thriving in an Age of Extinction* (New York: PublicAffairs, 2017), 53.

11 "Humans are in . . . as a whole.": M. R. O'Connor, *Resurrection Science: Conservation, De-extinction, and the Precarious Future of Wild Things* (New York: St. Martin's, 2015), 6.

11 "We are as . . . good at it.": Britt Wray, *Rise of the Necrofauna: The Science, Ethics, and Risks of De-extinction* (Vancouver, BC: Greystone, 2017), 5.

15 "This year's prize . . . code of life.": Katherine Wu, Carl Zimmer, and Elian Peltier, "Nobel Prize in Chemistry Awarded to 2 Scientists for Work on Genome Editing," *New York Times*, October 7, 2020, https://www.nytimes .com/2020/10/07/science/nobel-prize -chemistry-crispr.html.

15 "It was really . . . from the beginning.": "Jennifer Doudna's First Reactions to 2020 Nobel Prize Win," YouTube video, 10:00, posted by UC Berkeley, October 7, 2020, https://www.youtube.com/watch ?v=RbNI_V0P574/.

15 "It's kind of . . . safely and effectively.": Jennifer Doudna, quoted in "The Long View on Gene Editing," *Scientific American*, January 9, 2020, https://www .scientificamerican.com/custom -media/biggest-questions-in-science /the-long-view-on-gene-editing; "Jennifer Doudna's First Reactions," UC Berkeley.

26 "We never wanted . . . with hybridization.":
Annie Roth, "Scientists Accidentally Bred
the Fish Version of a Liger," *New York
Times*, July 15, 2020, https://www
.nytimes.com/2020/07/15/science
/hybrid-sturgeon-paddlefish.html.

27 Introgression is "prolific.": Jordana
Cepelewicz, "Interspecies Hybrids Play a
Vital Role in Evolution," Quanta, August
24, 2017, https://www.quantamagazine
.org/interspecies-hybrids-play-a-vital-role
-in-evolution-20170824.

27 "Increasingly evidence is . . . even modern
humans.": Shubhobroto Ghosh, Piyali
Chattopadhyay Sinha, and Anindya
Sinha, "The Litigon Rediscovered:
Implications for Biological Species
Concept and Value Systems in Science,"
Nature India, April 12, 2017, https://
doi10.1038/nindia.2017.46.

28 "capable of freely . . . itself *in nature*.":
Edward O. Wilson, *The Diversity of Life*
(New York: W. W. Norton, 1999), xii.

29 "Nature produces individuals . . .
of individuals collectively.": Nina V.
Fedoroff and Nancy Marie Brown,
*Mendel in the Kitchen: A Scientist's View of
Genetically Modified Foods* (Washington,
DC: Joseph Henry, 2004), 68.

29 "merely artificial combinations . . . the
term species.": Charles Darwin, *On the
Origin of Species by Means of Natural
Selection* (London: John Murray, 1859),
485, https://en.wikisource.org/wiki
/On_the_Origin_of_Species_(1859).

31 "my favorite animal . . . skills in magic.":
Napoleon Dynamite, directed by Jared
Hess (Century City, CA: Fox Searchlight
Pictures, 2004).

34 "threatens the 'genetic identity' of
wolves.": "Wolf-Dog 'Swarms' Threaten
Europe's Wolves," *Frontiers Science
News*, September 5, 2019, https://blog

.frontiersin.org/2019/09/05/ecology
-evolution-wolf-dog-hybrids.

37 "What protection . . . 50 percent coyote?":
Sarah Zhang, "The Secret Identity of a
Coyote-like Creature," *Atlantic*, November
8, 2019, https://www.theatlantic.com
/science/archive/2019/11/the-ghost-genes
-of-a-nearly-extinct-animal-live-on-in
-texas/601624/.

38 "the idea that . . . hybridization is
ludicrous": Thomas, *Inheritors of the
Earth*, 195.

39 "Given how much . . . million years ago.":
Thomas, 151.

42 "The new genetic . . . change
everything.": Torill Kornfeldt, *The
Re-origin of Species: A Second Chance for
Extinct Animals*, trans. Fiona Graham
(London: Scribe, 2018), 112.

46 "to reassemble them . . . unscrambling an
egg.": Wilson, *The Diversity of Life*, xxiv.

49 "Speciation by hybridization . . . of
the Anthropocene.": Wray, *Rise of the
Necrofauna*, 68.

51 "The thing is . . . or drought-resistant.":
Kornfeldt, *The Re-origin of Species*, 117.

51–52 "emblematic of the . . . using old
methods.": Kornfeldt, 35–36.

52 "Why should we . . . to avoid losses?":
Thomas, *Inheritors of the Earth*, 9.

53 "This technology doesn't . . . us being
human.": Kornfeldt, *The Re-origin of
Species*, 117.

57 "What is the . . . a wild population?":
Beth Shapiro, *How to Clone a Mammoth:
The Science of De-extinction* (Princeton,
NJ: Princeton University Press, 2015), 25.

59 "what we would . . . 'em back alive.":
Jack Horner and James Gorman, *How
to Build a Dinosaur: Extinction Doesn't
Have to Be Forever* (New York: Dutton,
2009), 5.

59 "Dinosaurs never did . . . in their genome.": Horner and Gorman, 115.

60 "reverse the evolutionary . . . a dinosaur instead.": Kornfeldt, *The Re-origin of Species*, 177.

60 "The fundamental reason . . . how it works.": Horner and Gorman, *How to Build a Dinosaur*, 193.

61 "Changes in the . . . changes in evolution.": Horner and Gorman, 139.

61 "On the evolutionary . . . in different ways.": Horner and Gorman, 149.

61 "all living things . . . of a continuum.": Horner and Gorman, 9.

62 "If you follow . . . for hot sauce.": Horner and Gorman, 9.

63 "we could stuff . . . says, like chicken.": Horner and Gorman, 174.

63 "fair to the . . . and well-functioning.": Horner and Gorman, 174, 206.

63 "We've made all . . . to be me.": Kornfeldt, *The Re-origin of Species*, 184.

67 "animals have created . . . is slowly increasing.": "History of the Park," Pleistocene Park, accessed November 25, 2019, https://www.pleistocenepark.ru.

67 "What we've shown . . . simple, inexpensive solution": Kornfeldt, *The Re-origin of Species*, 198.

67 "We're bringing back . . . is a success.": Nathaniel Rich, "The New Origin of Species," *New York Times Magazine*, March 2, 2014, 27.

68 "We will never . . . of a mammoth.": Shapiro, *How to Clone*, 11.

68 "we can . . . resurrect . . . their extinct traits": Shapiro, 10.

69 "a cold-resistant . . . the same ecosystem.": "The Mammoth," Colossal, accessed September 26, 2021, https://colossal.com/mammoth.

69 "programmable molecular scalpel": *Unnatural Selection*, directed by Leeor Kaufman and Joe Egender, aired October 18, 2019, on Netflix, https://www.netflix.com/title/80208910.

69 "We might be . . . of old ones.": Kornfeldt, *The Re-origin of Species*, 31, 117.

72 "no longer be . . . the Old World.": Shapiro, *How to Clone*, 207.

72 "to save species . . . from becoming extinct." Diane Toomey, "Cloning a Mammoth: Science Fiction or Conservation Tool?," Yale Environment 360, June 17, 2005, https://e360.yale.edu/features/cloning_a_mammoth_science_fiction_or_conservation_tool.

72 "Mammoth hemoglobin . . . surviving cold environments": "Why Bring Back the Woolly Mammoth?," Revive & Restore, accessed November 25, 2019, https://reviverestore.org/projects/woolly-mammoth.

72 "Certainly, if we . . . certainly not smooth.": Shapiro, *How to Clone*, xi.

78 "will look like . . . like an aurochs.": Ronald Goderie et al., *The Aurochs: Born to Be Wild; The Comeback of a European Icon* (Zutphen, Netherlands: Roodbont, 2013), 118.

78 "We want to . . . twenty-first century.": Kornfeldt, *The Re-origin of Species*, 141.

80 "We're talking about . . . would be finished.": Kornfeldt, 146.

80–81 "An aurochs is . . . with remarkable kindness.": Cis van Vuure, *Retracing the Aurochs: History, Morphology, and Ecology of an Extinct Wild Ox*, trans. KHM van den Berg (Sofia, Bulgaria: Pensoft, 2005), 93.

84 "A new passenger . . . far from over.": Ben Novak, "Reflections on Martha's Centennial," Revive & Restore, September 1, 2014, https://reviverestore.org/of-martha-the-last-passenger-pigeon.

84 "aerial evolutions . . . a gigantic serpent": Joel Greenberg, *A Feathered River across the Sky: The Passenger Pigeon's Flight to Extinction* (New York: Bloomsbury, 2014), 155.

84 "passes like a thought.": Tim Flannery and Peter Schouten, *A Gap in Nature: Discovering the World's Extinct Animals* (New York: Atlantic Monthly, 2001), 124.

84 "Never have my . . . meteors from heaven.": Greenberg, *A Feathered River across the Sky*, 52.

84 "a biological storm," "feathered tempest": Greenberg, 129.

86 "quite possibly is . . . eastern United States.": "Passenger Pigeon Project," Revive & Restore, accessed March 4, 2021, https://reviverestore.org/about-the -passenger-pigeon.

87 "the world's first . . . pigeon germline chimera.": "Progress to Date: 2019 Updates," Revive & Restore, accessed March 4, 2021, https://reviverestore.org /projects/the-great-passenger-pigeon -comeback/progress-to-date.

87 "It's their behavior . . . we'll have failed.": Kornfeldt, *The Re-origin of Species*, 55.

88 "a perfect scourge . . . every sprouting plant.": Greenberg, *A Feathered River across the Sky*, 41, 76.

90 "significant underestimate": "Summary Statistics," IUCN Red List, accessed February 20, 2020, http://www .iucnredlist.org/about/summary -statistics#How_many_threatened.

93 "Our civilization rests . . . instead of grass.": Fedoroff and Brown, *Mendel in the Kitchen*, x.

96 "is as safe . . . made from clones.": "A Primer on Cloning and Its Use in Livestock Operations," US Food and Drug Administration, updated August 29, 2018, https://www.fda.gov/animal

-veterinary/animal-cloning/primer -cloning-and-its-use-livestock-operations.

96 "an identical twin born later": Eric Mortenson, "To Clone, or Not to Clone," Salem (OR)_Capital Press, August 25, 2016, https://www.capitalpress.com /ag_sectors/livestock/to-clone-or-not-to -clone/article_c2872e5d-45fe-565d-91a3 -d63a776ce539.html.

99 "perfectly healthy": "A Primer on Cloning and Its Use in Livestock Operations," US Food and Drug Administration.

102 "I had the . . . I was wrong.": Andrew Pollack, "Move to Market Gene-Altered Pigs in Canada Is Halted," *New York Times*, April 3, 2012, https://www .nytimes.com/2012/04/04/science/gene -altered-pig-project-in-canada-is-halted .html.

106 "super pig . . . produce less excretions.": Alison Van Eenennaam, "Two Pendulous Nipples," *Biobeef Blog*, January 1, 2018, https://biobeef.faculty.ucdavis.edu/2018 /01.

109 "It is as . . . a tomato 'fishy.'": Fedoroff and Brown, *Mendel in the Kitchen*, 94.

111 "Our fish was . . . land-based farming.": Chuck Goudie and Christine Tressel, "Genetically Modified Fish to Eat Growing in the Midwest," ABC News, July 22, 2019, https://abc7chicago.com /food/genetically-modified-fish-to-eat -growing-in-the-midwest/5412062/.

112 "Regulation is important . . . is absolutely nonsensical.": Megan Molteni, "Spilled Milk," Undark, June 30, 2016, https:// undark.org/article/gmo-goats-lysozyme -uc-davis-diarrhea; Ann Hess, "Is the Pork Industry Stuck between a Rock and a Hard Place?," National Hog Farmer, January 25, 2019, https://www .nationalhogfarmer.com/business/pork -industry-stuck-between-rock-and-hard -place.

112 "no biologically relevant differences": "AquAdvantage Salmon Fact Sheet," US Food & Drug Administration, updated August 5, 2019, https://www.fda.gov/animal-veterinary/animals-intentional-genomic-alterations/aquadvantage-salmon-fact-sheet.

113 "extremely low likelihood": "AquAdvantage Salmon."

114 "In twenty or . . . modified animal products.": Richard Martin, "One Fish, Two Fish, Strange Fish, New Fish," bioGraphic, February 13, 2018, https://www.biographic.com/one-fish-two-fish-strange-fish-new-fish.

115 "The challenge of . . . use them wisely.": Fedoroff and Brown, *Mendel in the Kitchen*, xiii.

117 "the opportunity to . . . of synthetic biology.": International Genetically Engineered Machine Competition (iGEM), accessed March 4, 2021, https://www.igem.org.

123 "GFP is used . . . a test tube.": Marc Zimmer, *Glowing Genes: A Revolution in Biotechnology* (Amherst, NY: Prometheus Books, 2005), 105.

123 "I will never . . . her well-being.": Eduardo Kac, "GFP Bunny," accessed January 20, 2020, https://www.ekac.org/gfpbunny.html.

124–125 "a serious debate . . . human and nonhumankind.": Kac.

125 "How can I . . . rabbit at home?": Eduardo Kac, "Alba Guestbook (2000)," accessed January 20, 2020, http://www.ekac.org/bunnybook.2000.html.

131 "I opened a . . . are just crazy.": Stanley Coren, "A Designer Dog-Maker Regrets His Creation," *Psychology Today*, April 1, 2014, https://www.psychologytoday.com/us/blog/canine-corner/201404/designer-dog-maker-regrets-his-creation.

131 "There are a . . . very, very few.": Coren.

137 "liked to sit . . . smell the flowers.": Munro Leaf, *The Story of Ferdinand* (New York: Puffin Books, 1977), 8.

138 "I guess he's been reincarnated": John Woestendiek, *Dog, Inc.: The Uncanny Inside Story of Cloning Man's Best Friend* (New York: Avery, 2010), 65.

138 "like a light . . . get easily aggravated.": Woestendiek, 171.

139 "Chance was one . . . one didn't get.": Woestendiek, 173.

139 "different personalities . . . and her seriousness.": Matt Stevens, "Barbra Streisand Cloned Her Dog. For $50,000, You Can Clone Yours," *New York Times*, February 28, 2018, https://www.nytimes.com/2018/02/28/science/barbra-streisand-clone-dogs.html.

140 "America's most trusted animal cloning company": Scott Neuman, "Send in the Clones: Barbra Streisand Reveals Fluffy Canine Copies," NPR, February 28, 2018, https://www.npr.org/sections/thetwo-way/2018/02/28/589404560/send-in-the-clones-barbra-streisand-reveals-fluffy-canine-copies; ViaGen Pets, accessed February 4, 2020, https://www.viagenpets.com.

140 "It does seem . . . conventionally bred litters.": Maureen McKinney, "Pet Cloning: Where We Are Today," American Veterinarian, November 18, 2018, https://www.americanveterinarian.com/journals/amvet/2018/november2018/pet-cloning-where-we-are-today.

141 "People who love . . . a breeding machine.": Jessica Pierce, "Cloning Pets: Just One Bad Idea after Another," *Psychology Today*, February 20, 2016, https://www.psychologytoday.com/blog/all-dogs-go-heaven/201602/cloning-pets.

144 "breathable skin protection," "an antiwrinkle ingredient": Alex Scott, "Delivering on Spider Silk's Promise," *Chemical & Engineering News* 95, no. 8 (February 20, 2017), https://cen.acs.org/articles/95/i8/Delivering-spider-silks-promise.html.

146 "the world's first commercially available cyborg": "The RoboRoach Bundle," Backyard Brains, accessed January 24, 2020, https://backyardbrains.com/products/roboroach.

148 "reckless experimentation . . . and ethical norms.": Jennifer Doudna, "He Jiankui," Time 100, *Time*, accessed February 18, 2020, https://time.com/collection/100-most-influential-people-2019/5567707/he-jiankui/.

149 "Should we use . . . far stronger species?": Zoltan Istvan, quoted in Mark O'Connell, "The Immortality Campaign," *New York Times Magazine*, February 12, 2017.

154 "no adverse effects . . . eggs as normal.": "Hen Eggs with Human Proteins Offer Drug Hope," Roslin Institute, August 12, 2019, https://www.ed.ac.uk/roslin/news-events/latest-news/archive/2019/hen-eggs-human-proteins-drug-hope.

154 "can produce in . . . literally chicken feed.": "Anti-Cancer Chicken Eggs Produced," BBC, January 14, 2007, http://news.bbc.co.uk/2/hi/science/nature/6261427.stm.

155 "Every human in . . . clearly not toxic.": Molteni, "Spilled Milk."

155 "At present, we are on hold": Heidi Ledford, "Gene-Edited Animal Creators Look beyond US Market," *Nature* 566, no. 7745 (February 21, 2019), https://www.nature.com/articles/d41586-019-00600-4.

156 "I've got someone . . . the first egg.": Sara Reardon, "Welcome to the CRISPR Zoo," *Nature* 531, no. 7593 (March 9, 2016), https://www.nature.com/news/welcome-to-the-crispr-zoo-1.19537.

157 "a modern tragedy . . . the precautionary principle.": Ed Regis, "Golden Rice: The Imperiled Birth of a GMO Superfood," Johns Hopkins University Press, October 3, 2019, https://www.press.jhu.edu/news/blog/golden-rice-imperiled-birth-gmo-superfood.

164 "more robust": Kelly Servick, "Study on DNA Spread by Genetically Modified Mosquitoes Prompts Backlash," *Science*, September 17, 2019, https://www.sciencemag.org/news/2019/09/study-dna-spread-genetically-modified-mosquitoes-prompts-backlash.

165 "it has become . . . to our extinction.": Bryan Walsh, *End Times: A Brief Guide to the End of the World* (New York: Hachette Books, 2019), 210.

169 "prolonged survival": Bruno Reichart et al., "Pig-to-Non-Human Primate Heart Transplantation: The Final Step toward Clinical Xenotransplantation?," *Journal of Heart and Lung Transplantation* 39, no. 8 (August 1, 2020): 751–757, https://www.jhltonline.org/article/S1053-2498(20)31556-4/fulltext.

169 "that it now . . . transplantation is feasible": Massachusetts General Hospital, "Hearts Harvested from Pigs May Soon Help Solve Chronic Shortage of Organs," press release, October 7, 2020, https://www.massgeneral.org/news/press-release/Hearts-harvested-from-pigs-may-soon-help-solve-chronic-shortages-of-these-donor-organs.

170 "will pave the . . . lungs, or livers.": Emily Mullin, "Surgeons Are Transplanting Genetically Engineered Pig Skin onto Humans," OneZero, November 11, 2019, https://onezero .medium.com/surgeons-transplanted -pig-skin-onto-humans-for-the-first -time-607fc519eb56.

170 "It was better . . . a living donor.": Roni Caryn Rabin, "In a First, Surgeons Attached a Pig Kidney to a Human, and It Worked," *New York Times*, October 19, 2021, https://www.nytimes .com/2021/10/19/health/kidney -transplant-pig-human.html.

172 "How we define . . . value of life.": John D. Loike, "Opinion: Should Human-Animal Chimeras Be Granted 'Personhood'?" *Scientist*, May 23, 2018, https://www.the -scientist.com/news-opinion/opinion -should-human-animal-chimeras-be -granted-personhood-36664.

177 "detectable genetic material . . . found in nature": "BE Disclosure," USDA, accessed March 4, 2021, https://www .ams.usda.gov/rules-regulations/be.

BIBLIOGRAPHY

INTRODUCTION

Anthes, Emily. *Frankenstein's Cat: Cuddling Up to Biotech's Brave New Beasts*. New York: Scientific American/Farrar, Straus & Giroux, 2013.

Brockman, John, ed. *Know This: Today's Most Interesting and Important Scientific Ideas, Discoveries, and Developments*. New York: Harper Perennial, 2017.

Fedoroff, Nina V., and Nancy Marie Brown. *Mendel in the Kitchen: A Scientist's View of Genetically Modified Foods*. Washington, DC: Joseph Henry, 2004.

Hubbell, Sue. *Shrinking the Cat: Genetic Engineering before We Knew about Genes*. Boston: Houghton Mifflin, 2001.

Kornfeldt, Torill. *The Re-origin of Species: A Second Chance for Extinct Animals*. Translated by Fiona Graham. London: Scribe, 2018.

"The Long View on Gene Editing." *Scientific American*, January 9, 2020. https:// www.scientificamerican.com/custom-media/biggest-questions-in-science/the-long -view-on-gene-editing.

O'Connor, M. R. *Resurrection Science: Conservation, De-extinction, and the Precarious Future of Wild Things*. New York: St. Martin's, 2015.

Shapiro, Beth. *How to Clone a Mammoth: The Science of De-extinction*. Princeton, NJ: Princeton University Press, 2015.

Thomas, Chris D. *Inheritors of the Earth: How Nature Is Thriving in an Age of Extinction*. New York: PublicAffairs, 2017.

Unnatural Selection. Directed by Leeor Kaufman and Joe Egender. Aired October 18, 2019, on Netflix. https://www.netflix.com/title/80208910.

Wilson, Edward O. *The Diversity of Life*. New York: W. W. Norton, 1999.

Wohlsen, Marcus. *Biopunk: DIY Scientists Hack the Software of Life*. New York: Current, 2011.

Wray, Britt. *Rise of the Necrofauna: The Science, Ethics, and Risks of De-extinction*. Vancouver, BC: Greystone, 2017.

Zimmer, Marc. *Glowing Genes: A Revolution in Biotechnology*. Amherst, NY: Prometheus Books, 2005.

CHAPTER 1 LIGERS, TIGONS & LITIGONS

Bittel, Jason. "Hold Your Zorses: The Sad Truth about Animal Hybrids." *Slate*, June 19, 2015. https://slate.com/technology/2015/06/zonkeys-ligers-the-sad-truth-about -animal-hybrids.html.

Cepelewicz, Jordana. "Interspecies Hybrids Play a Vital Role in Evolution." Quanta, August 24, 2017. https://www.quantamagazine.org/interspecies-hybrids-play-a-vital -role-in-evolution-20170824.

Choi, Charles Q. "Liger and Tigons, Oh My! Cat Lineage Littered with Interbreeding." Live Science, January 15, 2016. https://www.livescience.com/53389-cat-lineage-littered -with-interbreeding.html.

Garnett, Stephen T., and Les Christidis. "Taxonomy Anarchy Hampers Conservation." *Nature* 546 (June 1, 2017): 25–27.

Ghosh, Shubhobroto, Piyali Chattopadhyay Sinha, and Anindya Sinha. "The Litigon Rediscovered: Implications for Biological Species Concept and Value Systems in Science." *Nature India*, April 12, 2017. http://doi10.1038/nindia.2017.46.

Hall, Jani. "Cat Experts: Ligers and Other Designer Hybrids Pointless and Unethical." *National Geographic*, February 24, 2017. https://www.nationalgeographic.com/news /2017/02/wildlife-watch-liger-tigon-big-cat-hybrid.

"Largest Living Cat." *Guinness World Records*. Accessed August 12, 2021. https:// www.guinnessworldrecords.com/world-records/largest-living-cat.

"The Liger." *Liger Facts*. Accessed August 12, 2021. https://www.ligerfacts.org.

"Liger." Wikipedia. Accessed August 12, 2021. https://en.wikipedia.org/wiki/Liger.

"List of Genetic Hybrids." Wikipedia. Accessed August 12, 2021. https://en.wikipedia .org/wiki/List_of_genetic_hybrids.

Milman, Oliver. "Ligers and Tigons: Activists Aim to Outlaw 'Inhumane' Breeding of Frankencats." *Guardian* (US edition), May 19, 2017. https://www.theguardian.com/world/2017/may/19/frankencats-breeding-inhumane-usda-petition.

"*Panthera* Hybrid." Wikipedia. Accessed August 12, 2021. https://en.wikipedia.org/wiki/Panthera_hybrid.

Roth, Annie. "Scientists Accidentally Bred the Fish Version of a Liger." *New York Times*, July 15, 2020. https://www.nytimes.com/2020/07/15/science/hybrid-sturgeon-paddlefish.html.

Singer, Emily. "As Animals Mingle, a Baffling Genetic Barrier." Quanta, August 5, 2014. https://www.quantamagazine.org/how-a-tiny-chunk-of-dna-can-keep-two-species-apart-20140805.

Velasquez-Manoff, Moises. "Lions and Tigers and Bears, Oh My!" *New York Times Magazine*, August 17, 2014, 32–37.

Wilson, Edward O. *The Diversity of Life*. New York: W. W. Norton, 1999.

CHAPTER 2 COYWOLVES, RED WOLVES & WOLF DOGS

Beeland, T. DeLene. *The Secret World of Red Wolves*. Chapel Hill: University of North Carolina Press, 2013.

Busch, Robert H. *The Wolf Almanac: A Celebration of Wolves and Their World*. Guilford, CT: Lyons, 2007.

Keim, Brandon. "Some Wolves Are on Their Way to Domestication—Again." *Anthropocene*, April 12, 2017. http://www.anthropocenemagazine.org/2017/04/modern-wolf-domestication.

Mech, David, and Luigi Boitani, eds. *Wolves: Behavior, Ecology, and Conservation*. Chicago: University of Chicago Press, 2003.

Petersen, Bo. "Only 14 Red Wolves Remain in SC Wild, and US Agency Won't Say What They're Doing about It." *Charleston (SC) Post and Courier*, October 16, 2019. https://www.postandcourier.com/news/only-red-wolves-remain-in-sc-wild-and-us-agency/article_86e4b19c-ef61-11e9-a3bf-bbe391f97381.html.

"Red Wolf." Federal Wildlife Service. Accessed August 12, 2021. https://www.fws.gov/southeast/wildlife/mammals/red-wolf.

Thomas, Chris D. *Inheritors of the Earth: How Nature Is Thriving in an Age of Extinction*. New York: PublicAffairs, 2017.

Velasquez-Manoff, Moises. "Lions and Tigers and Bears, Oh My!" *New York Times Magazine*, August 17, 2014, 32–37.

"Wolf-Dog 'Swarms' Threaten Europe's Wolves." *Frontiers Science News*, September 5, 2019. https://blog.frontiersin.org/2019/09/05/ecology-evolution-wolf-dog-hybrids.

Zhang, Sarah. "The Secret Identity of a Coyote-like Creature." *Atlantic*, November 8, 2019. https://www.theatlantic.com/science/archive/2019/11/the-ghost-genes-of-a-nearly-extinct-animal-live-on-in-texas/601624.

CHAPTER 3 RHINOS: BLACK, WHITE & GRAY

Adams, Douglas, and Mark Carwardine. *Last Chance to See*. New York: Harmony Books, 1991.

Anderson Sam. "The Last Two Northern White Rhinos on Earth." *New York Times Magazine*, January 6, 2021. https://www.nytimes.com/2021/01/06/magazine/the-last-two-northern-white-rhinos-on-earth.html.

Anthony, Lawrence, and Graham Spence. *The Last Rhinos: My Battle to Save One of the World's Greatest Creatures*. New York: Thomas Dunne Books, 2012.

Cunningham, Carol, and Joel Berger. *Horn of Darkness: Rhinos on the Edge*. New York: Oxford University Press, 1997.

Fortin, Jacey. "Scientists Fertilize Eggs from the Last Two Northern White Rhinos." *New York Times*, August 28, 2019. https://www.nytimes.com/2019/08/28/science/northern-white-rhino-eggs-fertilized.html.

"Happy End to a Challenging Year: Two New Northern White Rhino Embryos Created at Christmas—Now There Are Five." Leibniz Institute for Zoo & Wildlife Research Berlin, January 14, 2021. http://www.biorescue.org/en/news/happy-end-challenging-year-two-new-northern-white-rhino-embryos-created-christmas-now-there.

Imbler, Sabrina. "Meet Elizabeth Ann, the First Cloned Black-Footed Ferret." *New York Times*, February 18, 2021. https://www.nytimes.com/2021/02/18/science/black-footed-ferret-clone.html.

Nuwer, Rachel. "Sudan, the Last Male Northern White Rhino, Dies in Kenya." *New York Times*, March 20, 2018. https://www.nytimes.com/2018/03/20/science/rhino-sudan-extinct.html.

O'Connor, M. R. *Resurrection Science: Conservation, De-extinction, and the Precarious Future of Wild Things*. New York: St. Martin's, 2015.

Player, Ian. *The White Rhino Saga*. New York: Stein and Day, 1973.

Shapiro, Beth. *How to Clone a Mammoth: The Science De-extinction*. Princeton, NJ: Princeton University Press, 2015.

Wray, Britt. *Rise of the Necrofauna: The Science, Ethics, and Risks of De-extinction*. Vancouver, BC: Greystone, 2017.

CHAPTER 4 PIZZLIES & NARLUGAS

Cepelewicz, Jordana. "Interspecies Hybrids Play a Vital Role in Evolution." Quanta, August 24, 2017. https://www.quantamagazine.org/interspecies-hybrids-play-a-vital-role-in-evolution-20170824.

"Grizzly-Polar Bear Hybrid." Wikipedia. Accessed August 12, 2021. https://en.wikipedia.org/wiki/Grizzly-polar_bear_hybrid.

Hall, Jani. "Cat Experts: Ligers and Other Designer Hybrids Pointless and Unethical." *National Geographic*, February 24, 2017. https://www.nationalgeographic.com/news/2017/02/wildlife-watch-liger-tigon-big-cat-hybrid.

Hsu, Charlotte. "Polar Bear Evolution Tracked Climate Change, New DNA Study Suggests." University of Buffalo, July 23, 2012. http://www.buffalo.edu/news/releases/2012/07/13548.html.

Kornfeldt, Torill. *The Re-origin of Species: A Second Chance for Extinct Animals*. Translated by Fiona Graham. London: Scribe, 2018.

Martin, Claire. "Brown Polar Bears, Beluga-Narwhals and Other Hybrids Brought to You by Climate Change." *Smithsonian*, March 22, 2013. https://www.smithsonianmag.com/science-nature/brown-polar-bears-beluga-narwhals-and-other-hybrids-brought-to-you-by-climate-change-7331236.

Milman, Oliver. "Pizzly or Grolar Bear: Grizzly-Polar Hybrid Is a New Result of Climate Change." *Guardian* (US edition), May 18, 2016. https://www.theguardian.com/environment/2016/may/18/pizzly-grolar-bear-grizzly-polar-hybrid-climate-change.

O'Connor, M. R. *Resurrection Science: Conservation, De-extinction, and the Precarious Future of Wild Things*. New York: St. Martin's, 2015.

Pennisi, Elizabeth. "Polar Bear Evolution Was Fast and Furious." *Science*, May 8, 2014. https://www.sciencemag.org/news/2014/05/polar-bear-evolution-was-fast-and-furious.

Preston, Elizabeth. "Tuskless Elephants Escape Poachers, but May Evolve New Problems." *New York Times*, October 21, 2021. https://www.nytimes.com/2021/10/21/science/tuskless-elephants-evolution.html.

"Supplementary Information to Kelly, B., Whiteley, A. & Tallmon, D. 'The Arctic Melting Pot.'" *Nature* 468, no. 891 (2010). https://doi10.1038/468891a.

Velasquez-Manoff, Moises. "Lions and Tigers and Bears, Oh My!" *New York Times Magazine*, August 17, 2014, 32–37.

Yong, Ed. "Narlugas Are Real." *Atlantic*, June 20, 2019. https://www.theatlantic.com/science/archive/2019/06/narluga-very-strange-hybrid-whale/592057.

CHAPTER 5 CHICKENOSAURUS

Biello, David. "Mutant Chicken Grows Alligatorlike Teeth." *Scientific American*, February 22, 2006. https://www.scientificamerican.com/article/mutant-chicken-grows-alli.

Geggel, Laurel. "Dino-Chicken Gets One Step Closer." Live Science, May 19, 2015. https://www.livescience.com/50886-scientific-progress-dino-chicken.html.

Horner, Jack, and James Gorman. *How to Build a Dinosaur: Extinction Doesn't Have to Be Forever*. New York: Dutton, 2009.

Kornfeldt, Torill. *The Re-origin of Species: A Second Chance for Extinct Animals*. Translated by Fiona Graham. London: Scribe, 2018.

Switek, Brian. "What Could Live in a Real Jurassic World? A Chickenosaurus." *National Geographic*, June 18, 2015. https://www.nationalgeographic.com/news/2015/06/150618-jurassic-world-genetic-engineering-chickenosaurus.

Weiss, Geoff. "Scientists Say They Can Recreate Living Dinosaurs within the Next Few Years." *Entrepreneur*, June 18, 2019. https://www.entrepreneur.com/article/247402.

CHAPTER 6 WOOLLY MAMMOTH

Anthes, Emily. *Frankenstein's Cat: Cuddling Up to Biotech's Brave New Beasts*. New York: Scientific American/Farrar, Straus & Giroux, 2013.

"Guiding Principles on Creating Proxies of Extinct Species for Conservation Benefit." International Union for Conservation of Nature (IUCN), May 18, 2016. https://portals.iucn.org/library/node/46248.

Kolata, Gina. "Scientists Grow Mouse Embryos in a Mechanical Womb." *New York Times*, March 17, 2021. https://www.nytimes.com/2021/03/17/health/mice-artificial-uterus.html.

Kornfeldt, Torill. *The Re-origin of Species: A Second Chance for Extinct Animals*. Translated by Fiona Graham. London: Scribe, 2018.

Pleistocene Park. Accessed August 12, 2021. https://www.pleistocenepark.ru.

Rich, Nathaniel. "The New Origin of Species." *New York Times*, March 2, 2014.

Shapiro, Beth. *How to Clone a Mammoth: The Science of De-extinction*. Princeton, NJ: Princeton University Press, 2015.

"The Mammoth," Colossal, accessed September 26, 2021, https://colossal.com/mammoth.

"Woolly Mammoth Revival." Revive & Restore. Accessed August 12, 2021. https://reviverestore.org/projects/woolly-mammoth.

Wray, Britt. *Rise of the Necrofauna: The Science, Ethics, and Risks of De-extinction.* Vancouver, BC: Greystone, 2017.

Zimmer, Carl. "A New Company with a Wild Mission: Bring Back the Woolly Mammoth." *New York Times*, September 13, 2021. https://www.nytimes.com /2021/09/13/science/colossal-woolly-mammoth-DNA.html.

CHAPTER 7 AUROCHS/TAUROS

Breeding-Back Blog. Accessed August 12, 2021. http://breedingback.blogspot.com.

Dutch Tauros Programme. Accessed August 12, 2021. http://taurosprogramme.com.

Goderie, Ronald, Wouter Helmer, Henri Kerkdijk-Otten, and Staffan Widstrand. *The Aurochs: Born to Be Wild; The Comeback of a European Icon.* Zutphen, Netherlands: Roodbont, 2013.

Kornfeldt, Torill. *The Re-origin of Species: A Second Chance for Extinct Animals.* Translated by Fiona Graham. London: Scribe, 2018.

Rewilding Europe. Accessed August 12, 2021. https://rewildingeurope.com/rewilding -in-action/wildlife-comeback/tauros.

True Nature Foundation. Accessed August 12, 2021. http://truenaturefoundation.org.

Vuure, Cis van. *Retracing the Aurochs: History, Morphology, and Ecology of an Extinct Wild Ox.* Translated by KHM van den Berg. Sofia, Bulgaria: Pensoft, 2005.

Wray, Britt. *Rise of the Necrofauna: The Science, Ethics, and Risks of De-extinction.* Vancouver, BC: Greystone, 2017.

CHAPTER 8 PASSENGER PIGEONS

Brand, Stewart. "Rethinking Extinction." *Aeon*, April 21, 2015. https://aeon.co/essays /we-are-not-edging-up-to-a-mass-extinction.

Fuller, Errol. *The Passenger Pigeon.* Princeton, NJ: Princeton University Press, 2015.

Greenberg, Joel. *A Feathered River across the Sky: The Passenger Pigeon's Flight to Extinction.* New York: Bloomsbury, 2014.

Kornfeldt, Torill. *The Re-origin of Species: A Second Chance for Extinct Animals.* Translated by Fiona Graham. London: Scribe, 2018.

O'Connor, M. R. *Resurrection Science: Conservation, De-extinction, and the Precarious Future of Wild Things.* New York: St. Martin's, 2015.

"Passenger Pigeon Project." Revive & Restore. Accessed August 12, 2021. https://reviverestore.org/about-the-passenger-pigeon.

Shapiro, Beth. *How to Clone a Mammoth: The Science of De-extinction*. Princeton, NJ: Princeton University Press, 2015.

FROZEN ARKS: CRYOBANKING ON THE FUTURE
Frozen Ark Project. Accessed August 12, 2021. http://frozenark.org.

Frozen Zoo at the San Diego Zoo. Accessed August 12, 2021. https://institute .sandiegozoo.org/resources/frozen-zoo%C2%AE.

Vertebrate Genomes Project. Accessed November 3, 2021. https://vertebrategenomes project.org.

Kornfeldt, Torill. *The Re-origin of Species: A Second Chance for Extinct Animals*. Translated by Fiona Graham. London: Scribe, 2018.

O'Connor, M. R. *Resurrection Science: Conservation, De-extinction, and the Precarious Future of Wild Things*. New York: St. Martin's, 2015.

Pan-Smithsonian Cryo-Initiative. Accessed August 12, 2021. https://www.si.edu/psci.

"Summary Statistics." International Union for Conservation of Nature (IUCN) Red List. Accessed August 12, 2021. https://www.iucnredlist.org/about/summary -statistics#How_many_threatened.

Wray, Britt. *Rise of the Necrofauna: The Science, Ethics, and Risks of De-extinction*. Vancouver, BC: Greystone, 2017.

CHAPTER 9 DOLLY & THE CLONES
Anthes, Emily. *Frankenstein's Cat: Cuddling Up to Biotech's Brave New Beasts*. New York: Scientific American/Farrar, Straus & Giroux, 2013.

Compassion in World Farming. "Farm Animal Cloning." Accessed August 12, 2021. https://www.ciwf.org.uk/media/3816935/farm-animal-cloning-report.pdf.

Goodwin, Shan. "The Pros and Cons of Cloning Beef Animals." *Farm Online National*, September 7, 2017. https://www.farmonline.com.au/story/4908346/the -pros-and-cons-of-cloning-beef-animals.

Mortenson, Eric. "To Clone, or Not to Clone." *Salem (OR) Capital Press*. Updated December 13, 2018. https://www.capitalpress.com/ag_sectors/livestock/to-clone-or -not-to-clone/article_c2872e5d-45fe-565d-91a3-d63a776ce539.html.

"A Primer on Cloning and Its Use in Livestock Operations." US Food and Drug Administration. Updated August 29, 2018. https://www.fda.gov/animal-veterinary /animal-cloning/primer-cloning-and-its-use-livestock-operations.

Shapiro, Beth. *How to Clone a Mammoth: The Science of De-extinction*. Princeton, NJ: Princeton University Press, 2015.

Trans Ova Genetics. Accessed August 12, 2021. https://transova.com/service/cloning-services.

Wray, Britt. *Rise of the Necrofauna: The Science, Ethics, and Risks of De-extinction*. Vancouver, BC: Greystone, 2017.

CHAPTER 10 SUPER PIGS & HORNLESS CATTLE

Arnason, Robert. "China Develops an 'Enviro-Pig.'" *Western Producer*, June 7, 2018. https://www.producer.com/2018/06/china-develops-an-enviro-pig.

Barber, Gregory. "A More Humane Livestock Industry, Brought to You by Crispr." *Wired*, March 18, 2019. https://www.wired.com/story/crispr-gene-editing-humane-livestock.

Bloch, Sam. "Hornless Holsteins and Enviropigs: The Genetically Engineered Animals We Never Knew." *New Food Economy*, May 1, 2018. https://newfoodeconomy.org/transgenesis-gene-editing-fda-aquabounty.

Choi, Candice. "Farm Animals May Soon Get New Features through Gene Editing." Phys.org, November 15, 2018. https://phys.org/news/2018-11-farm-animals-features-gene.html.

Harmon, Amy. "Open Season Is Seen in Gene Editing of Animals." *New York Times*, November 26, 2015. https://www.nytimes.com/2015/12/22/science/gene-drives-offer-new-hope-against-diseases-and-crop-pests.html.

Hess, Ann. "Is the Pork Industry Stuck between a Rock and a Hard Place?" *National Hog Farmer*, January 25, 2019. https://www.nationalhogfarmer.com/business/pork-industry-stuck-between-rock-and-hard-place.

Hubbell, Sue. *Shrinking the Cat: Genetic Engineering before We Knew about Genes*. Boston: Houghton Mifflin, 2001.

Peterson, Hayley. "Calm Down, Rumors about KFC Mutant Chickens Are Not Real." *Business Insider*, February 28, 2014. https://www.businessinsider.com/kfc-mutant-chickens-are-not-real-2014-2.

Pollack, Andrew. "Move to Market Gene-Altered Pigs in Canada Is Halted." *New York Times*, April 3, 2012. https://www.nytimes.com/2012/04/04/science/gene-altered-pig-project-in-canada-is-halted.html.

Tai-Burkard, Christine, Andrea Doeschl-Wilson, Mike J. McGrew, Alan L. Archibald, Helen M. Sang, Ross D. Houston, C. Bruce Whitelaw, and Mick Watson. "Livestock 2.0—Genome Editing for Fitter, Healthier, and More Productive Farmed Animals." *Genome Biology* 19, no. 204 (November 2018). https://genomebiology.biomedcentral.com/articles/10.1186/s13059-018-1583-1.

Traubman, Tamara. "The Naked Truth about the Naked Chicken." *Haaretz* (Tel Aviv, Israel), May 23, 2002. https://www.haaretz.com/israel-news/culture/1.5186919.

Van Eenennaam, Alison. "Two Pendulous Nipples." *Biobeef Blog*, January 1, 2018. https://biobeef.faculty.ucdavis.edu/2018/01.

CHAPTER 11 FRANKENFISH

Anthes, Emily. *Frankenstein's Cat: Cuddling Up to Biotech's Brave New Beasts*. New York: Scientific American/Farrar, Straus & Giroux, 2013.

AquaBounty. Accessed August 12, 2021. https://www.aquabounty.com.

"AquAdvantage Salmon Fact Sheet." US Food & Drug Administration. Updated August 5, 2019. https://www.fda.gov/animal-veterinary/animals-intentional-genomic -alterations/aquadvantage-salmon-fact-sheet.

Barber, Gregory. "A More Humane Livestock Industry, Brought to You by Crispr." *Wired*, March 18, 2019. https://www.wired.com/story/crispr-gene-editing-humane -livestock.

Bloch, Sam. "America's Biggest Retailers and Foodservice Companies Have Already Agreed Not to Sell GMO Salmon." *Counter*, February 11, 2021. https://thecounter.org /americas-biggest-retailers-foodservice-companies-gmo-salmon-aquabounty.

Bloch, Sam. "Hornless Holsteins and Enviropigs: The Genetically Engineered Animals We Never Knew." *New Food Economy*, May 1, 2018. https://newfoodeconomy .org/transgenesis-gene-editing-fda-aquabounty.

Fedoroff, Nina V., and Nancy Marie Brown. *Mendel in the Kitchen: A Scientist's View of Genetically Modified Foods*. Washington, DC: Joseph Henry, 2004.

Goudie, Chuck, and Christine Tressel. "Genetically Modified Fish to Eat Growing in the Midwest." ABC News, July 22, 2019. https://abc7chicago.com/food/genetically -modified-fish-to-eat-growing-in-the-midwest/5412062.

Hubbell, Sue. *Shrinking the Cat: Genetic Engineering before We Knew about Genes*. Boston: Houghton Mifflin, 2001.

Johnson, Carolyn Y. "Gene-Edited Farm Animals Are Coming. Will We Eat Them?" *Washington Post*, December 17, 2018. https://www.washingtonpost.com/news/national /wp/2018/12/17/feature/gene-edited-farm-animals-are-coming-will-we-eat-them.

Martin, Richard. "One Fish, Two Fish, Strange Fish, New Fish." *bioGraphic*, February 13, 2018. https://www.biographic.com/one-fish-two-fish-strange-fish-new-fish.

Molteni, Megan. "Spilled Milk." Undark, June 30, 2016. https://undark.org/article /gmo-goats-lysozyme-uc-davis-diarrhea.

Pollack, Andrew. "Genetically Engineered Salmon Approved for Consumption." *New York Times*, November 19, 2015. https://www.nytimes.com/2015/11/20/business /genetically-engineered-salmon-approved-for-consumption.html.

Regalado, Antonio. "Gene-Edited Cattle Have a Major Screwup in Their DNA." *MIT Technology Review*, August 29, 2019. https://www.technologyreview.com/s/614235 /recombinetics-gene-edited-hornless-cattle-major-dna-screwup.

Smith, Casey, Associated Press. "First Shipments of Genetically Modified Salmon Go to Restaurants in Eastern US." *Anchorage Daily News*, June 1, 2021. https://www.adn .com/business-economy/2021/06/01/genetically-modified-salmon-head-to-restaurants -in-eastern-us.

US Food & Drug Administration. "FDA Approves First-of-Its-Kind Intentional Genomic Alteration in Line of Domestic Pigs for Both Human Food, Potential Therapeutic Uses." Press release, December 14, 2020. https://www.fda.gov/news -events/press-announcements/fda-approves-first-its-kind-intentional-genomic -alteration-line-domestic-pigs-both-human-food.

Van Eenennaam, Alison. "Regulation of Genetically Modified Animals Part #1." *Biobeef Blog*, December 28, 2020. https://biobeef.faculty.ucdavis.edu/2020/12/28 /regulation-of-genetically-modified-animals-part-1.

Wohlsen, Marcus. *Biopunk: DIY Scientists Hack the Software of Life*. New York: Current, 2011.

Zimmer, Marc. *Glowing Genes: A Revolution in Biotechnology*. Amherst, NY: Prometheus Books, 2005.

SYNTHETIC BIOLOGY: DIY REVOLUTION OR DISASTER?

Anthes, Emily. *Frankenstein's Cat: Cuddling Up to Biotech's Brave New Beasts*. New York: Scientific American/Farrar, Straus & Giroux, 2013.

Church, George, and Ed Regis. *Regenesis: How Synthetic Biology Will Reinvent Nature and Ourselves*. New York: Basic Books, 2012.

DIYbio. Accessed August 12, 2021. https://www.diybio.org.

International Genetically Engineered Machine Competition (iGEM). Accessed August 12, 2021. http://www.igem.org.

Walsh, Bryan. *End Times: A Brief Guide to the End of the World*. New York: Hachette Books, 2019.

Wohlsen, Marcus. *Biopunk: DIY Scientists Hack the Software of Life*. New York: Current, 2011.

Wray, Britt. *Rise of the Necrofauna: The Science, Ethics, and Risks of De-extinction*. Vancouver, BC: Greystone, 2017.

CHAPTER 12 MR. GREEN GENES

Anthes, Emily. *Frankenstein's Cat: Cuddling Up to Biotech's Brave New Beasts*. New York: Scientific American/Farrar, Straus & Giroux, 2013.

Giaimo, Cara. "Meet the Newest Member of the Fluorescent Mammal Club." *New York Times*, February 18, 2021. https://www.nytimes.com/2021/02/18/science/fluorescent-mammal-springhare.html.

Giaimo, Cara. "More Mammals Are Hiding Their Secret Glow." *New York Times*, December 18, 2020. https://www.nytimes.com/2020/12/18/science/glowing-mammals-australia.html.

GloFish. Accessed August 12, 2021. https://www.glofish.com.

Greenwood, Veronique. "Flying Squirrels That Glow Pink in the Dark." *New York Times*, February 1, 2019. https://www.nytimes.com/2019/02/01/science/pink-squirrels-glow.html.

Kac, Eduardo. "GFP Bunny." Accessed August 12, 2021. https://www.ekac.org/gfpbunny.html.

Philipkoski, Kristen. "RIP: Alba, the Glowing Bunny." *Wired*, August 12, 2002. https://www.wired.com/2002/08/rip-alba-the-glowing-bunny.

Woestendiek, John. *Dog, Inc.: The Uncanny Inside Story of Cloning Man's Best Friend*. New York: Avery, 2010.

Wohlsen, Marcus. *Biopunk: DIY Scientists Hack the Software of Life*. New York: Current, 2011.

Zimmer, Marc. *Glowing Genes: A Revolution in Biotechnology*. Amherst, NY: Prometheus Books, 2005.

CHAPTER 13 DESIGNER DOGS, CUSTOM CATS & TEACUP PIGS

Anthes, Emily. *Frankenstein's Cat: Cuddling Up to Biotech's Brave New Beasts*. New York: Scientific American/Farrar, Straus & Giroux, 2013.

Coren, Stanley. "A Designer Dog-Maker Regrets His Creation." *Psychology Today*, April 1, 2014. https://www.psychologytoday.com/us/blog/canine-corner/201404/designer-dog-maker-regrets-his-creation.

Cyranoski, David. "Gene-Editing 'Micropigs' to Be Sold as Pets at Chinese Institute." *Nature* 526, no. 7571 (September 29, 2015). https://www.nature.com/news/gene-edited-micropigs-to-be-sold-as-pets-at-chinese-institute-1.18448.

Parletta, Natalie. "Doxiepoos and Puggles: Is Hybrid Breeding Healthier for Owners and Dogs?" *Guardian* (US edition), October 23, 2019. https://www.theguardian.com /lifeandstyle/2019/oct/24/doxiepoos-and-puggles-is-hybrid-breeding-healthier-for -owners-and-dogs.

Pinkstone, Joe. "First Genetically Engineered Super Horse, Designed to Be Faster and Stronger, Could Be Born in 2019." *Daily Mail* (London), December 27, 2017. https:// www.dailymail.co.uk/sciencetech/article-5214753/Genetically-engineered-super -horses-win-Olympics.html.

Reardon, Sara. "Welcome to the CRISPR Zoo." *Nature* 531, no. 7593 (March 9, 2016). https://www.nature.com/news/welcome-to-the-crispr-zoo-1.19537.

Regalado, Antonio. "First Gene-Edited Dogs Reported in China." *MIT Technology Review*, October 19, 2015. https://www.technologyreview.com/s/542616/first-gene -edited-dogs-reported-in-china.

Rueb, Emily S., and Niraj Chokshi. "Labradoodle Creator Says the Breed Is His Life's Regret." *New York Times*, September 25, 2019. https://www.nytimes.com/2019/09/25 /us/labradoodle-creator-regret.html.

Sheridan, Kate. "Don't Hold Your Breath for Allergy-Free Cats." *MIT Technology Review*, July 19, 2018. https://www.technologyreview.com/s/611671/dont-hold-your -breath-for-allergy-free-cats.

Standaert, Michael. "China Genomics Giant Drops Plans for Gene-Edited Pets." *MIT Technology Review*, July 3, 2017. https://www.technologyreview.com/s/608207/china -genomics-giant-drops-plans-for-gene-edited-pets.

Woestendiek, John. *Dog, Inc.: The Uncanny Inside Story of Cloning Man's Best Friend.* New York: Avery, 2010.

CHAPTER 14 [INSERT YOUR PET'S NAME HERE]

Anthes, Emily. *Frankenstein's Cat: Cuddling Up to Biotech's Brave New Beasts.* New York: Scientific American/Farrar, Straus & Giroux, 2013.

Bell, Ryan. "Game of Clones." Outside, December 10, 2013. https://www .outsideonline.com/outdoor-adventure/game-clones.

Cohen, Jon. "Six Cloned Horses Help Rider Win Prestigious Polo Match." *Science*, December 13, 2016. https://www.sciencemag.org/news/2016/12/six-cloned-horses -help-rider-win-prestigious-polo-match.

"Dog Cloning at Sooam." Sooam Biotech Research Foundation. Accessed August 12, 2021. http://en.sooam.com/dogcn/sub01.html.

McKinney, Maureen. "Pet Cloning: Where We Are Today." *American Veterinarian,*

November 18, 2018. https://www.americanveterinarian.com/journals/amvet/2018/november2018/pet-cloning-where-we-are-today.

PerPETuate. Accessed August 12, 2021. https://www.perpetuate.net.

Pierce, Jessica. "Cloning Pets: Just One Bad Idea after Another." *Psychology Today*, February 20, 2016. https://www.psychologytoday.com/blog/all-dogs-go-heaven/201602/cloning-pets.

Shapiro, Beth. *How to Clone a Mammoth: The Science of De-extinction*. Princeton, NJ: Princeton University Press, 2015.

ViaGen Pets. Accessed August 12, 2021. https://www.viagenpets.com.

Woestendiek, John. *Dog, Inc.: The Uncanny Inside Story of Cloning Man's Best Friend*. New York: Avery, 2010.

CHAPTER 15 SPIDER GOATS, REMOTE-CONTROL ROACHES & RAT CYBORGS

Ackerman, Evan. "Draper's Genetically Modified Cyborg DragonflEye Takes Flight." IEEE Spectrum, June 1, 2017. https://spectrum.ieee.org/automaton/robotics/industrial-robots/draper-dragonfleye-project.

Andrews, Bill. "Researchers Create 'Rat Cyborgs' That People Control with Their Minds." *Discover*, February 14, 2019. https://www.discovermagazine.com/technology/researchers-create-rat-cyborgs-that-people-control-with-their-minds#.XOmNqVNKi-o.

Anthes, Emily. *Frankenstein's Cat: Cuddling Up to Biotech's Brave New Beasts*. New York: Scientific American/Farrar, Straus & Giroux, 2013.

Brockman, John, ed. *Know This: Today's Most Interesting and Important Scientific Ideas, Discoveries, and Developments*. New York: Harper Perennial, 2017.

Greene, Sean. "Using Lasers, Scientists Turn Mice into Ferociously Efficient Hunters." *Los Angeles Times*, January 18, 2017. https://www.latimes.com/science/sciencenow/la-sci-sn-mice-hunters-brain-20170118-story.html.

Hubbell, Sue. *Shrinking the Cat: Genetic Engineering before We Knew about Genes*. Boston: Houghton Mifflin, 2001.

Maharbiz, Michel M., and Hirotaka Sato. "Cyborg Beetles: Merging of Machine and Insect to Create Flying Robots." *Scientific American*, December 2010. https://www.scientificamerican.com/article/cyborg-beetles.

Martyn-Hemphill, Richard. "What Happened to Those GM Spider Goats with the Silky Milk?" *AG Funder News*, September 2, 2019. https://agfundernews.com/what-happened-to-those-gm-spider-goats-with-the-silky-milk.html.

Murphy, Debra. "The Intricacies of Spinning Spider Silk Strands Out of Goat Milk," *Genome Alberta*, January 6, 2015. http://genomealberta.ca/livestock/the-intricacies-of-spinning-spider-silk-strands-out-of-goat-milk.aspx.

"The RoboRoach Bundle." Backyard Brains. Accessed August 12, 2021. https://backyardbrains.com/products/roboroach.

Sample, Ian. "Cockroach Robots? Not Nightmare Fantasy but Science Lab Reality." *Guardian* (US edition), March 3, 2015. https://www.theguardian.com/science/2015/mar/04/cockroach-robots-not-nightmare-fantasy-but-science-lab-reality.

Scott, Alex. "Delivering on Spider Silk's Promise." *Chemical & Engineering News* 95, no. 8 (February 20, 2017). https://cen.acs.org/articles/95/i8/Delivering-spider-silks-promise.html.

BRAVE NEW US: IMPROVING HUMANS

Brockman, John, ed. *Know This: Today's Most Interesting and Important Scientific Ideas, Discoveries, and Developments*. New York: Harper Perennial, 2017.

Cohen, Jon. "China's CRISPR Push in Animals Promises Better Meat, Novel Therapies, and Pig Organs for People." *Science*, July 31, 2019. https://www.sciencemag.org/news/2019/07/china-s-crispr-push-animals-promises-better-meat-novel-therapies-and-pig-organs-people.

Cyranoski, David. "What CRISPR-Baby Prison Sentences Mean for Research." *Nature* 577 (January 3, 2020). https://www.nature.com/articles/d41586-020-00001-y.

Institute for Ethics and Emerging Technologies (IEET). Accessed August 12, 2021. https://www.ieet.org.

Kotler, Steven. *Tomorrowland: Our Journey from Science Fiction to Science Fact*. New York: Houghton Mifflin Harcourt, 2015.

O'Connell, Mark. "The Immortality Campaign." *New York Times*, February 12, 2017.

SENS (Strategies for Engineered Negligible Senescence) Research Foundation. Accessed August 12, 2021. https://www.sens.org.

Unnatural Selection. Directed by Leeor Kaufman and Joe Egender. Aired October 18, 2019, on Netflix. https://www.netflix.com/title/80208910.

Walsh, Bryan. *End Times: A Brief Guide to the End of the World*. New York: Hachette Books, 2019.

Wohlsen, Marcus. *Biopunk: DIY Scientists Hack the Software of Life*. New York: Current, 2011.

Wray, Britt. *Rise of the Necrofauna: The Science, Ethics, and Risks of De-extinction*. Vancouver, BC: Greystone, 2017.

CHAPTER 16 MEDICINAL GOATS & CHICKENS

Anthes, Emily. *Frankenstein's Cat: Cuddling Up to Biotech's Brave New Beasts*. New York: Scientific American/Farrar, Straus & Giroux, 2013.

"Anti-Cancer Chicken Eggs Produced." *BBC*, January 14, 2007. http://news.bbc.co.uk /2/hi/science/nature/6261427.stm.

Barber, Gregory. "A More Humane Livestock Industry, Brought to You by Crispr." *Wired*, March 18, 2019. https://www.wired.com/story/crispr-gene-editing-humane -livestock.

Bloch, Sam. "Hornless Holsteins and Enviropigs: The Genetically Engineered Animals We Never Knew." *New Food Economy*, May 1, 2018. https://newfoodeconomy .org/transgenesis-gene-editing-fda-aquabounty.

"Diarrhea: Common Illness, Global Killer." Centers for Disease Control and Prevention. Accessed February 15, 2020. https://www.cdc.gov/healthywater/pdf /global/programs/Globaldiarrhea508c.pdf.

Ledford, Heidi. "Gene-Edited Animal Creators Look beyond US Market." *Nature*, February 21, 2019. https://www.nature.com/articles/d41586-019-00600-4.

Molteni, Megan. "Spilled Milk," Undark, June 30, 2016. https://undark.org/article /gmo-goats-lysozyme-uc-davis-diarrhea.

Reardon, Sara. "Welcome to the CRISPR Zoo." *Nature* 531, no. 7593 (March 9, 2016). https://www.nature.com/news/welcome-to-the-crispr-zoo-1.19537.

Regis, Ed. "Golden Rice: The Imperiled Birth of a GMO Superfood." Johns Hopkins University Press, October 3, 2019. https://www.press.jhu.edu/news/blog/golden-rice -imperiled-birth-gmo-superfood.

CHAPTER 17 MOSQUITOS AGAINST MALARIA

Bates, Claire. "Would It Be Wrong to Eradicate Mosquitoes?" *BBC*, January 28, 2016. http://www.bbc.com/news/magazine-35408835.

Brockman, John, ed. *Know This: Today's Most Interesting and Important Scientific Ideas, Discoveries, and Developments*. New York: Harper Perennial, 2017.

Callaway, Ewen. "US Defense Agencies Grapple with Gene Drives." *Scientific American*, July 24, 2017. https://www.scientificamerican.com/article/u-s-defense -agencies-grapple-with-gene-drives.

Elflein, John. "Zika Virus—Statistics & Facts." Statista, February 18, 2019. https://www.statista.com/topics/3002/zika-virus-disease.

Filosa, Gwen. "It Could be Mosquito vs. Mosquito in the Keys to Combat Dengue and Zika." *Miami Herald*, September 13, 2019. https://www.miamiherald.com/news/local/community/florida-keys/article234970452.html.

Florida Keys Mosquito Control District. Accessed August 12, 2021. https://keysmosquito.org.

Kindhauser, Mary Kay, Tomas Allen, Veronika Frank, Ravi Shankar Santhana, and Christopher Dye. "Zika: The Origin and Spread of a Mosquito-Borne Virus." World Health Organization, April 18, 2016. https://www.who.int/publications/m/item/zika-the-origin-and-spread-of-a-mosquito-borne-virus.

Kornfeldt, Torill. *The Re-origin of Species: A Second Chance for Extinct Animals.* Translated by Fiona Graham. London: Scribe, 2018.

Kotler, Steven. *Tomorrowland: Our Journey from Science Fiction to Science Fact.* New York: Houghton Mifflin Harcourt, 2015.

Osterholm, Michael T. "How Scared Should You Be about Zika?" *New York Times*, January 29, 2016. https://www.nytimes.com/2016/01/31/opinion/sunday/zika-mosquitoes-and-the-plagues-to-come.html.

Oxitec. Accessed August 12, 2021. https://www.oxitec.com.

Pollack, Andrew. "New Weapon to Fight Zika: The Mosquito." *New York Times*, January 30, 2016. https://www.nytimes.com/2016/01/31/business/new-weapon-to-fight-zika-the-mosquito.html.

Reardon, Sara. "Welcome to the CRISPR Zoo." *Nature* 531, no. 7593 (March 9, 2016). https://www.nature.com/n.ews/welcome-to-the-crispr-zoo-1.19537.

Rosner, Hillary. "Tweaking Genes to Save Species." *New York Times*, April 16, 2016. http://www.nytimes.com/2016/04/17/opinion/sunday/tweaking-genes-to-save-species.html.

Serr, Megan. "Mice as Conservationists?" *Scientific American*, March 8, 2017. https://blogs.scientificamerican.com/guest-blog/mice-as-conservationists.

Unnatural Selection. Directed by Leeor Kaufman and Joe Egender. Aired October 18, 2019, on Netflix. https://www.netflix.com/title/80208910.

Wade, Nicholas. "Gene Drives Offer New Hope against Diseases and Crop Pests." *New York Times*, December 21, 2015. https://www.nytimes.com/2015/12/22/science/gene-drives-offer-new-hope-against-diseases-and-crop-pests.html.

World Mosquito Program. Accessed August 12, 2021. https://www.worldmosquito
program.org.

Wray, Britt. *Rise of the Necrofauna: The Science, Ethics, and Risks of De-extinction*.
Vancouver, BC: Greystone, 2017.

CHAPTER 18 PIGS WITH HUMAN HEARTS

Anthes, Emily. *Frankenstein's Cat: Cuddling Up to Biotech's Brave New Beasts*. New
York: Scientific American/Farrar, Straus & Giroux, 2013.

Chen, Angus. "Baboons Survive for Half a Year after Heart Transplants from Pigs."
Scientific American, December 5, 2018. https://www.scientificamerican.com/article
/baboons-survive-for-half-a-year-after-heart-transplants-from-pigs.

Cohen, Jon. "China's CRISPR Push in Animals Promises Better Meat, Novel Therapies, and
Pig Organs for People." *Science*, July 31, 2019. https://www.sciencemag.org/news2019/07
/china-s-crispr-push-animals-promises-better-meat-novel-therapies-and-pig-organs-people.

Koplin, Julian J., and Julian Savulescu. "Time to Rethink the Law on Part-Human
Chimeras." *Journal of Law and the Biosciences* 6, no. 1 (October 2019). https://www
.ncbi.nlm.nih.gov/pmc/articles/PMC6813936.

Lanese, Nicoletta. "First Human-Monkey Chimeras Developed in China." *Scientist*,
August 5, 2019. https://www.the-scientist.com/news-opinion/first-humanmonkey
-chimeras-developedin-china--66231.

Loike, John D., and Robert Pollack. "Opinion: Develop Organoids, Not Chimeras,
for Transplantation." *Scientist*, October 1, 2019. https://www.the-scientist.com/critic
-at-large/opinion--develop-organoids--not-chimeras--for-transplantation-66460.

Mullin, Emily. "Surgeons Are Transplanting Genetically Engineered Pig Skin onto
Humans." OneZero, November 11, 2019. https://onezero.medium.com/surgeons
-transplanted-pig-skin-onto-humans-for-the-first-time-607fc519eb56.

Nonhuman Rights Project. Accessed August 12, 2021. https://www.nonhumanrights.org.

"Organ Donation Statistics." Organdonor.gov. Accessed February 17, 2020. https://
www.organdonor.gov/statistics-stories/statistics.html.

Perry, Caroline. "Pig Organs for Human Patients: A Challenge Fit for CRISPR." Wyss
Institute, May 30, 2018. https://wyss.harvard.edu/news/pig-organs-for-human-patients
-a-challenge-fit-for-crispr.

Rabin, Roni Caryn. "In a First, Surgeons Attached a Pig Kidney to a Human, and It
Worked." *New York Times*, October 19, 2021. https://www.nytimes.com/2021/10/19
/health/kidney-transplant-pig-human.html.

Reichart, Bruno, Matthias Langin, Julia Radan, Maren Mokelke, Ines Buttgereit, Jiawei Ying, Ann Kathrin Fresch, et al. "Pig-to-Non-Human Primate Heart Transplantation: The Final Step toward Clinical Xenotransplantation?" *Journal of Heart and Lung Transplantation* 39, no. 8 (August 1, 2020): 751–757. https://.jhltonline.org/article/S1053-2498(20)31556-4/fulltext.

Sebo, Jeff. "Should Chimpanzees Be Considered 'Persons'?" *New York Times*, April 7, 2018. https://www.nytimes.com/2018/04/07/opinion/sunday/chimps-legal-personhood.html.

Stein, Rob. "NIH Plans to Lift Ban on Research Funds for Part-Human, Part-Animal Embryos." NPR, August 4, 2016. http://www.npr.org/sections/health-shots/2016/08/04/488387729/nih-plans-to-lift-ban-on-research-funds-for-part-human-part-animal-embryos.

Tai-Burkard, Christine, Andrea Doeschl-Wilson, Mike J. McGrew, Alan L. Archibald, Helen M. Sang, Ross D. Houston, C. Bruce Whitelaw, and Mick Watson. "Livestock 2.0—Genome Editing for Fitter, Healthier, and More Productive Farmed Animals." *Genome Biology* 19, no. 204 (November 2018). https://genomebiology.biomedcentral.com/articles/10.1186/s13059-018-1583-1.

Wade, Nicholas. "New Prospects for Growing Replacement Organs in Animals." *New York Times*, January 25, 2017. https://www.nytimes.com/2017/01/26/science/chimera-stemcells-organs.html.

XenoTherapeutics. "From Pig to Patient: XenoTherapeutics Completes First Cohort of Patients in First US Clinical Trial of Live-Cell Xenotransplant; Evidence of Safety and Efficacy Allows for Accelerated Patient Enrollment." Press release, November 5, 2020. https://www.globenewswire.com/news-release/2020/11/05/2121200/0/en/From-Pig-to-Patient-XenoTherapeutics-Completes-First-Cohort-of-Patients-in-First-US-Clinical-Trial-of-Live-Cell-Xenotransplant-Evidence-of-Safety-and-Efficacy-Allows-for-Accelerate.html.

INDEX

PHOTO ACKNOWLEDGMENTS

Image credits: Nastasic/Getty Images, p. 7; Andrew Brookes/Getty Images, p. 14; ScreenProd/Photononstop/Alamy Stock Photo, p. 18; viktorio/Shutterstock.com, p. 23; Shawn Hamilton/Shutterstock.com, p. 25; YuriyMaltsev/Shutterstock.com, p. 30; mjurik/Shutterstock.com, p. 34; Mark Newman/Getty Images, p. 36; David C Stephens/Getty Images, p. 38; TONY KARUMBA/Getty Images, p. 41; Cathy Withers-Clarke/Shutterstock.com, p. 45; Philippe Clement/Getty Images, p. 48; dottedhippo/Getty Images, p. 50; Andrew_Howe/Getty Images, p. 60; Tim Graham/Getty Images, p. 62; Aunt_Spray/Getty Images, p. 66; SPUTNIK/Alamy Stock Photo, p. 68; LKW/Independent Picture Service, p. 70; Oriol Querol/Shutterstock.com, p. 71; Dominic Robinson/Alamy Stock Photo, p. 76; Milan Rybar/Shutterstock.com, p. 79; Robert Landau/Getty Images, p. 80; Courtesy of National Audubon Society, p. 83; Science History Images/Alamy Stock Photo, p. 85; LEON NEAL,LEON NEAL/AFP/Getty Images, p. 91; Michael Smith/Getty Images, p. 95; AP Photo/Paul Clements, p. 97; AP Photo/John Chadwick, p. 99; Moshe Milner/GPO/Getty Images, p. 101; Michael Short/Bloomberg/Getty Images, p. 105; AP Photo/Michael Conroy, pp. 110, 113; AP Photo/Yonhap, Choi Byung-kil, p. 122; AP Photo/KK, p. 124; Silk-stocking/Getty Images, p. 126; bytgndmedia/Shutterstock.com, p. 130; itsabreeze photography/Getty Images, p. 133; dpa picture alliance/Alamy Stock Photo, p. 134; Reuters/Alamy Stock Photo, pp. 138, 161; AP Photo/Ahn Young-joon, p. 141; Salaithip Chaimongkol/EyeEm/Getty Images, p. 143; AP Photo/Chattanooga Times Free Press, Tim Barber, p. 145; MediaNews Group/Boston Herald/Getty Images, p. 147; Colin McPherson/Sygma/Getty Images, p. 154; inga spence/Alamy Stock Photo, p. 156; Nature and Science/Alamy Stock Photo, p. 163; Nature Picture Library/Alamy Stock Photo, p. 163; AP Photo/Duane R. Miller, p. 167; PPL Therapeutics via BWP Media/Getty Images, p. 169.